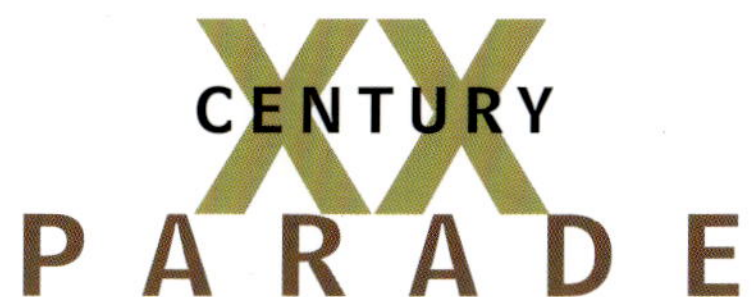

ARMANDO ROMERO

<table>
<tr><td>NEW YORK</td><td>DALLAS</td><td>LOS ANGELES</td></tr>
<tr><td>LESLIE FEELY FINE ART</td><td>THE MCKINNEY AVENUE
CONTEMPORARY/MAC</td><td>TASENDE GALLERY</td></tr>
<tr><td>MAY 7 – JUNE 6</td><td>MAY 9 – JUNE 20</td><td>MAY 14 – JUNE 20</td></tr>
</table>

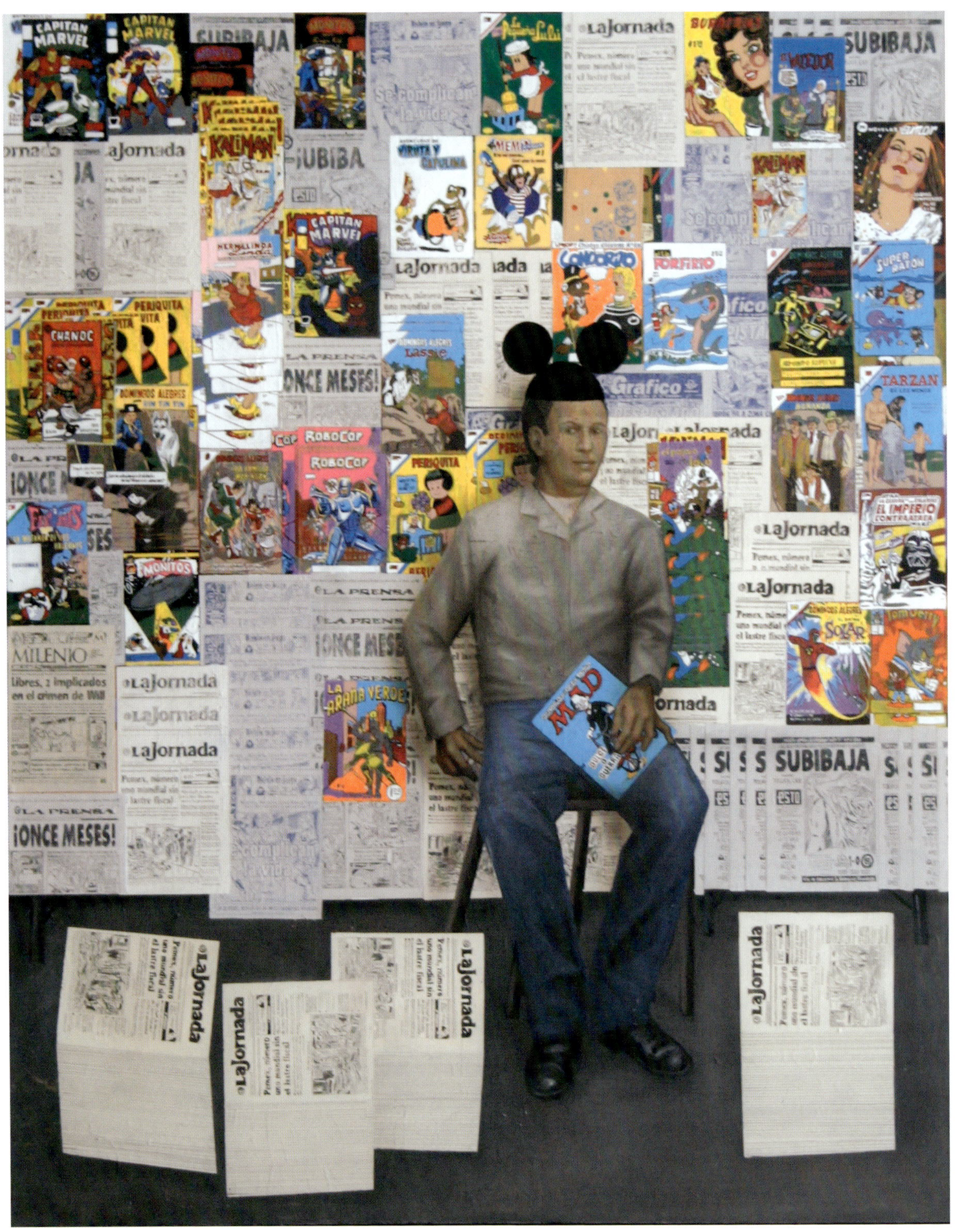

1 **La Jornada** 2008
Oil on wood panel
59 ¼ x 47 ¼ inches

We are awed by the gracious disposition and ability of the artist who produced this large body of work, 41 paintings and sculptures, during the last 18 months. Claude Albritton III of the McKinney Avenue Contemporary (The MAC) was the first to commit to the project and to display the larger works in the exhibition. The MAC's director Liliana Bloch has collaborated throughout with great enthusiasm and dedication. Leslie Feely later received the idea with much interest and her Manhattan gallery presents an important portion of *XX Century Parade*.

Three spaces nearly equal distance apart were necessary to accommodate the size of the exhibition and our desire to reach as many people as possible. It is our great pleasure to present Armando Romero's *XX Century Parade*.

MARY BETH PETERSEN
Director, Tasende Gallery

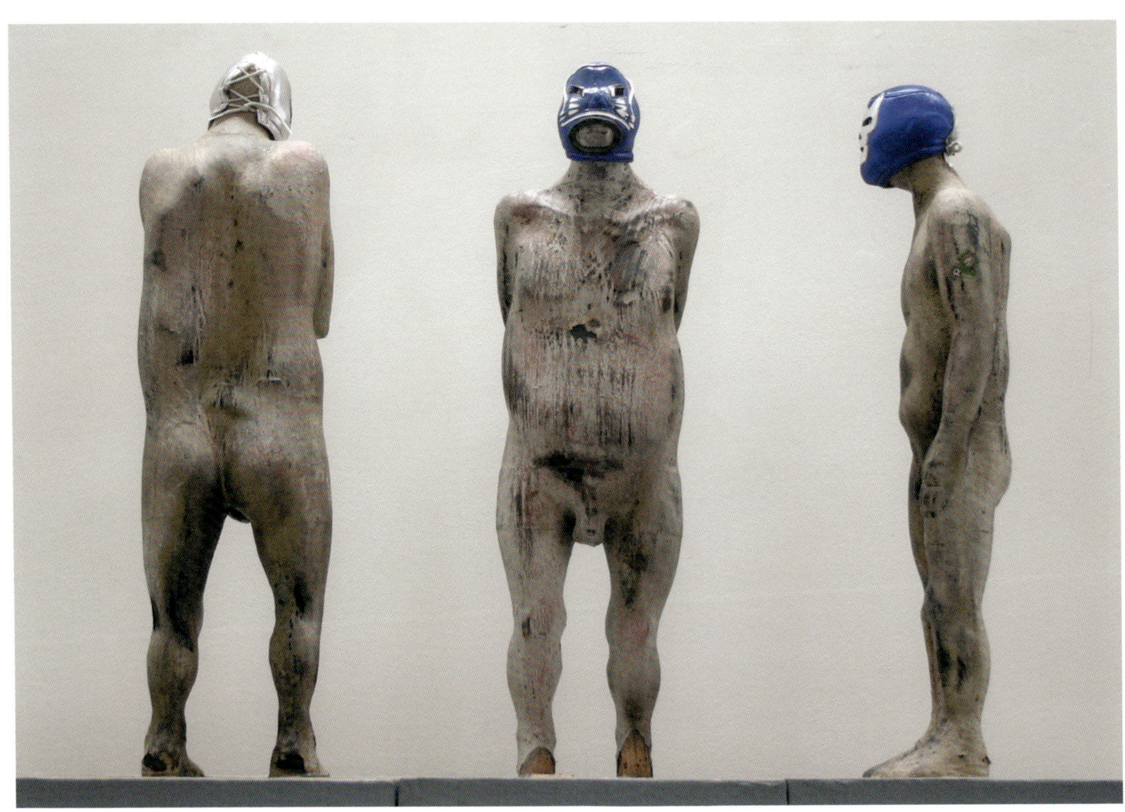

2 **Tres Tristes Tigres** 2008
Wood and vinyl, unique
24 x 9 7/8 x 11 1/8 inches; 24 x 9 ¾ x 9 5/8 inches; 24 ¾ x 9 7/8 x 11 1/8 inches

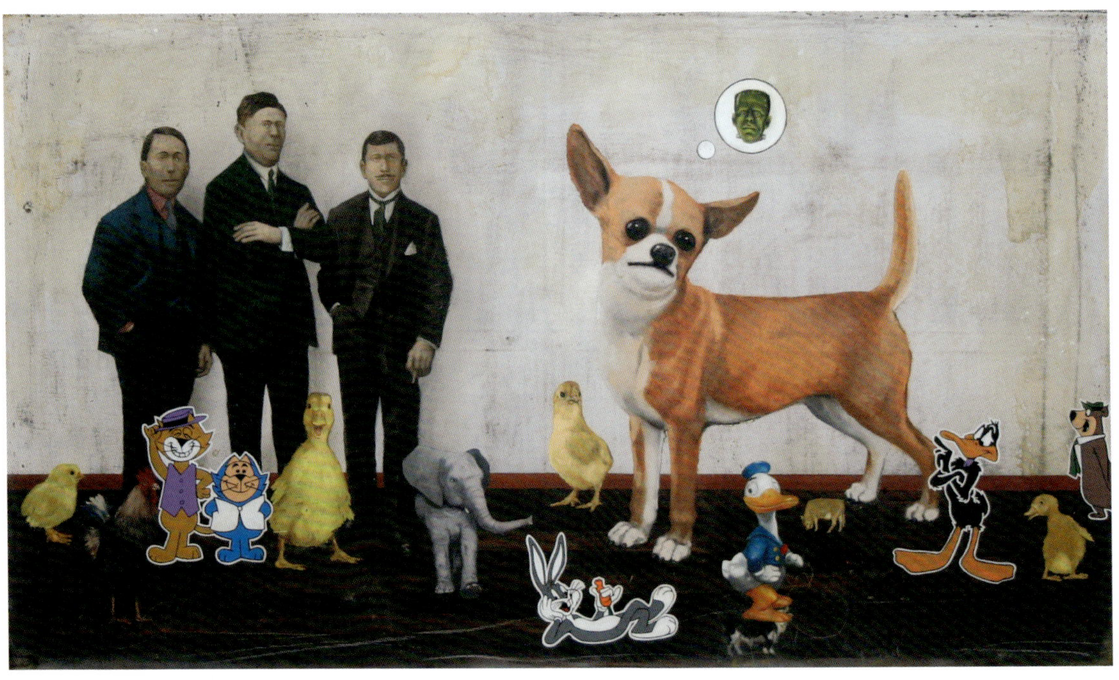

3 **Geneticists in Action** 2008
Oil on canvas
31 5/8 x 55 1/8 inches

THINKING ANEW THE IMITATION OF IMITATING: ARMANDO ROMERO'S XX CENTURY PARADE

CHARISSA N. TERRANOVA, PHD

Colliding image into image, Caravaggio into Kentucky Fried Chicken and Rembrandt into Foucault, the painter Armando Romero has been hailed a piercing postmodernist. His artful elision of quotation, layering, and trompe l'oeil – where Rosy the Robot, Big Boy, and Aunt Jemima crash the party of Veronese's *The Wedding at Cana* – would seem to make him rightful heir of postmodern schizophrenia and a keen illustrator of Jean Baudrillard's hyperreal.

Romero's most recent body of work, the paintings and sculptures in *XX Century Parade*, show him moving beyond the realm of postmodern quotation into new-millennium mimesis. Bearing patinas of false aging and tattered edges of pretended wear, paintings such as *Heroes of the Silver Screen* [fig 15] and *Dodgers* [fig 21] negotiate the imagistic spaces outside of the slick, science fiction suggestive of the hyperreal. Temporally speaking, they are images that do a dialectical three-step, forward to tomorrow then back to yesterday, and then a tiger's leap beyond into something altogether new. And they do so not by quoting something ideologically "original," paintings with the hallowed gravitas of an Old Master work or its historicist styling, but by mimicking the very act of mimesis itself.

The grey-toned *Heroes of the Silver Screen* offers a glimpse into what goes on behind the scenes of an old movie set and in the minds of the director, his aide, and a contemplative starlet. Though figures in monochrome, they think in color. With ironic aplomb, the elegantly clad actress thinks of the colorful pates of the Lion, Tin Man, and Scarecrow; the director those of The Three Stooges; and his aide, Dracula, Frankenstein, and the Werewolf. Process-wise, it looks prima facie to be a photorealist endeavor, a method in which the original would have been a small torn-edged old photograph, and its new rendering a large painted copy in grisaille. However this is not the case; the painting began as a painting, and an image born like Athena from the head of Romero. It is an amal-

gam, a rarefied glut in the artist's head of icons from the world of spectacles, an ersatz memory of a what-if photographic scene deconstructed to show the pop culture psyches of its characters. It is, in the most literal of terms, mimicking mimesis, acting out but not truly performing the work of copying since it is an original of Romero's own making.

While Romero's paintings are vibrant with the adulterations of the figural instead of the purities of abstraction, their logic calls upon the ideas of a great champion and philosopher of purist abstract painting. They recall what the twentieth-century critic Clement Greenberg described in 1939 as the "imitation of imitating." Greenberg probed Aristotle's thinking on imitation, or mimesis, and, in a brilliant sleight of hand transformed it from the copying of nature into the self-reflexive iteration of the logic of the medium of painting itself. In Part IV of Book I of the Poetics, Aristotle says that "imitation…is one instinct of our nature," and that it is our "natural gift." Later, in Part XXV of Book III, Aristotle gives great nuance to the way mimesis functions in the relationship between humans and nature. He tells us that while drawing upon nature by copying it, humans do better to improve upon what they see: "a probable impossibility is to be preferred to a thing improbable and yet possible. Again, it may be impossible that there should be men such as Zeuxis painted. 'Yes,' we say, 'but the impossible is the higher thing; for the ideal type must surpass the reality'." Greenberg inventively tweaks this idea for his own purposes, distilling the logic of mimesis in terms of abstract painting. In another essay from 1960, Greenberg would pithily describe this, his rationale of imitation, as "the use of characteristic methods of a discipline to criticize the discipline itself." Hence, modern painting marks the apotheosis of painting properly conceived: turned in upon itself, repetitively interrogating its process according to the application of paint to the surface of a square canvas, or Greenberg's sense of the "imitation of imitating."

If for Greenberg, the "imitation of imitating" meant distilling the essentials of the medium of painting in order to "entrench it more firmly in its area of competence," then for Romero it is to reveal that those essences are changeful phantasms constructed by manifold forces from the outside world. What Greenberg failed to realize and what Romero gets so well is that the "essences" of painting are historical. They change over time. Instead of hermetically sealing painting, these essences open it up and push it out into the world. A posteriori rather than a priori, the logic of painting for Romero is imaging: registering a world of prefabricated iconography, the icons of Old Masters as well as Hollywood and Looney Tunes.

Moving along in the three-step dialectic, Romero moves forward in conceptualizing an image, then goes back not to Greenberg's mimesis, but to Aristotle's, seemingly embracing its more literal sense of imitation. The third step occurs in the radical invention he performs with respect to Aristotelian mimesis. Similar to Greenberg, Romero tweaks Aristotelian mimesis for his own needs. He does not so much imitate a literal scene or image – a flower, tree, view of nature or cityscape, or their photographic renderings – but rather an ersatz copy of a scene or image, thereby reflecting the very logic of manufactured images. Romero's "imitation of imitating" reveals that memory and knowledge are constituted by images. Our thinking is fabricated through the mass production of images. Imitating not an actual photograph but an ersatz photograph, this doubling of mimesis, or the imitation of imitating, reflects the way images are made and amass in our minds, picture upon picture, kitschy stickers of cartoonish little leaguers atop the Americana of an old photo of a baseball team in *Dodgers*. Romero's imitation of imitating, that it seems as though he is copying but is replicating the act of copying, performs a critical commentary on the bombardment of images that we all experience on a daily basis and, in turn, the power we bestow upon and the magic we cathect into images. Images are the vehicle and substance of thinking and the creation of knowledge. As Aristotle tells us in *De Anima*, there is no thinking without images. The magic of phantasms, Romero's confabulation of pictures is thus the very stuff of thinking, in antiquity as well as our current moment.

Yet, the paintings in *Romero's XX Century Parade* appear literally imported from the past, and thus, upon first blush they seem more about the past than our present. Though feigned pictures of another era, rendered in realist fashion as though worked up in the 1930s, they poignantly comment on our own moment, in the process of imitating imitation but also in their content. Here I refer to the theme of genetic mishap and mutation at work in Romero's circus-world creatures. With light-hearted wit, *Taxidermist* [fig 19] pushes the envelope of creaturely confusion and curiosity. A stolid man, the taxidermist, sits amid an array of stuffed animals, colorful and fuzzy toys in varying proportions and sizes from a circus or fair. Behind him to the left, there is a vertical vitrine of "real" birds, dead, preserved and now on display. To his right a stuffed fabric toucan bird hangs mid-air; a lion and red bird sit below; and then on boxes and the floor there are Bambi, a teddy bear, small tiger, and baby version of the giant Chewbacca from Star Wars. Connecting taxidermy to genetics, stuffed animals both real and fake to the Promethean venture of manmade life, Romero has etched a fine white line, a string in the hands of the taxidermist, transforming him into puppeteer and would be Godlike creator.

Romero cross-examines in waggish and more incisive fashion the unlocking of the DNA code and genetic experimentation in the "Amazing Animal" series. In the bombast of circus-poster style, the backdrop of *Amazing Animal 2* [fig 8] shows a creature if not of confusion then of monstrous cross-wheeling. It has a cow's end, a tiger's trunk, and a wolf's head. Atop that we see carefully delineated in white line a German shepherd, perhaps Rin-Tin-Tin, the floating head of man, perhaps a scientist, the flattened form of pigs, a clown's beheaded body, and the scratch marks, also in white, of a vandal. It is an imagistic Babel of perverted form and manipulated nature. Used by writers immemorial, as in More's *Utopia*, Diderot's *Supplement au voyage de Bougainville*, and Bellamy's *Looking Backward*, the temporal and geographic far-away plays as a means to comment on the present. For Romero, painting as though in the 1930s provides critical distance, almost an Archimedean point, to comment on today's genetic sciences, everything from the bête noire of eugenics to premature puberty caused by hormone-saturated milk.

Humor is the constant that links work to work, painting to sculpture, in Romero's *XX Century Parade*. His is a strain of wit deep in its exploration of mishap, bodily un-fortune and the universal absurdity of life. Cast in bronze, the figures of *The Elephant* and *Clowns* share a certain strain of classical solemnity. In the former, the tiny cuteness of the elephant is tempered by the looming, heavy figures of two flanking clowns. In the latter, the three mound-like jesters of quotidian entertainment are more reminiscent of Rodin's *Balzac* than of Ronald McDonald. The wooden and vinyl *Tres Tristes Tigres* brings together the surface and screen-world pop culture of Lucha Libre, professional wrestling in Mexico, and the angst, sorrow, and uncertainty of the post-WW II modern sculpture of Giacometti and Picasso. Wearing superhuman blue and silver masks, three anonymous wrestlers stand smooth-bodied and vulnerable, one with arms behind him, the other with arms flaccidly to each side, and another arms crossed staunchly in front of him. They stand together yet divided in their body language.

As with Romero's paintings, the sculpture invokes a laughter driven by the farce of what we see and the subtle anxiousness that follows. It is a humor powered by an existential guffaw – laughter at life's meaning manufactured circus-like from the contradictory follies of pop culture and its forefather, putative western civilization.

Greenberg, Clement, "Avant-garde and Kitsch," 1939, http://www.sharecom.ca/greeberg/kitsch.html.

Aristotle, Poetics, http://classics.mit.edu/Aristotle/poetics.1.1.html.

Aristotle, Poetics, http://classics.mit.edu/Aristotle/poetics.3.3.html.

Greenberg, Clement, "Modernist Painting," 1960, http://www.sharecom.ca/greenberg/modernism.html.

Sepper, Dennis L., *Descarte's Imagination: Proportion, Images, and the Activity of Thinking* (Berkeley, CA: University of California Press, 1996) 18.

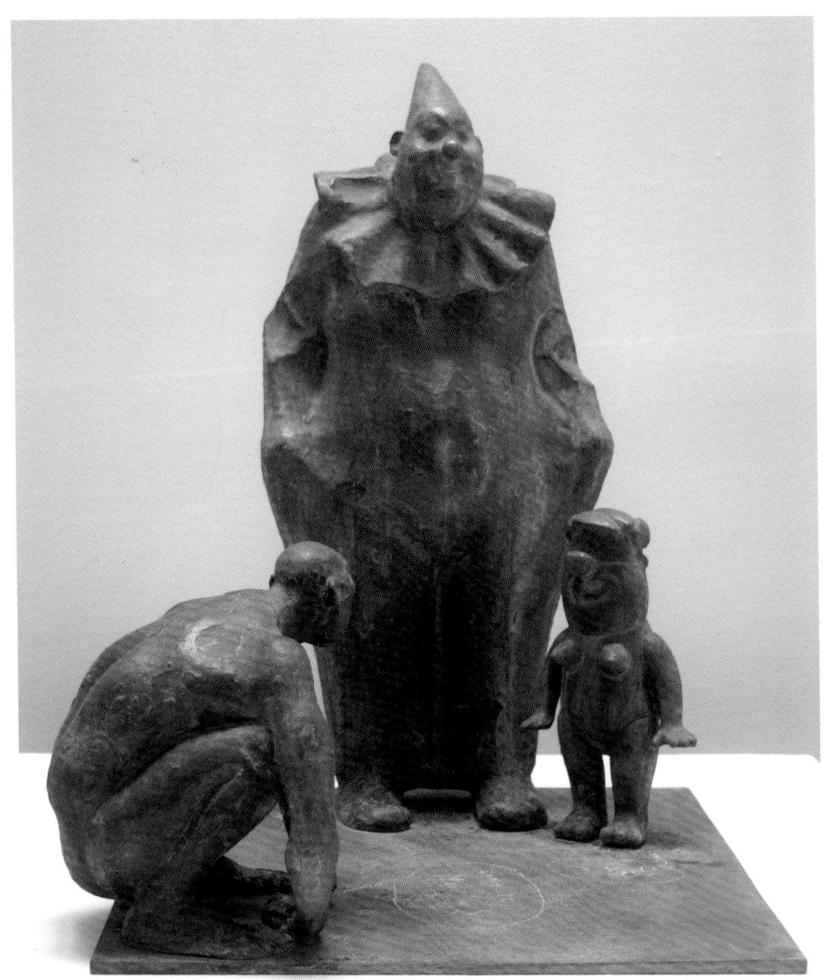

4 **Scene in the Ring** 2008
Bronze, unique
18 ½ x 16 ½ x 15 inches

TWENTIETH CENTURY

The Belle Epoch brings the Old and New Worlds together in Paris, the Germans have already been there many times before. Everything promises to be much larger and luxurious; the colossal replaces good taste and moderation. First the railways and later Henry Ford give the new century an unusual dynamism and a touch of glamour with which the middle class seeks to hide its vulgarity. Charles Lindbergh jumps over a huge puddle without splashing anyone. Meanwhile, science and investigation continue their assured ascension toward discoveries aimed at satisfying a nearly insatiable desire for progress. Achievements also make possible the Great War, which twenty-two years later is diminished by the political follies of a couple of polyphasic and inept painters. Sixty million dead. Meanwhile, on the other side of the planet the atom bomb ends the massacre between two countries separated by a pacific ocean. Later on, nuclear energy provides us with light as well as fear of complete darkness, all the while the beaches are clad in bikinis. To the rhythm of the Tango and Rock and Roll, the political geography of the planet is altered by every new conflict and the map changes colors every decade. Dogmatic charlatans posing as philosophers infiltrate the every day lives of entire countries advocating absurd theories that eventually fail due to Economics. All advancements disseminate their successes more easily thanks to new forms of communication, and public recognition is one of the most sought after trophies. Art could not remain on the fringe of the promotional benefits offered by the new century. Airwaves help music to conquer space and gain followers while painting and sculpture, together with the press boosted by improved methods of diffusion, look for new roads: *L'Ecole de Paris, Cubism, Surrealism, Expressionism, Socialist Realism, Abstract Expressionism, Muralism* and *Pop*. First it was the radio, then the great art of our time, film, followed by television. One of us walks on the moon. It's a world of contradictions, an immense stage of sporting competitions, and an enormous circus with a thousand rings where we are all clowns. The public is the protagonist and the spectator. The great banquet of numbers has begun and success is measured, as well as the inhabitants of planet Earth, the pill notwithstanding, in the billions for the first time. Finally, just like those before it, the twentieth century comes to a close, as Madoff makes his preparations for a festive party. At the dawn of the new millennium certain distinguished and brilliant philanthropists are being entertained by the greatest host.

In spite of the adoration to the masses, the tyranny of the numbers and the benefits all of this affords the defenders of mediocrity, the past century has provided individuals who excel and surge like prodigious plants fighting in the jungle against the underbrush. Nothing is easy. Some, like Erza Pound succumb in spite of genius. A beautiful woman named Leni Riefensthal seeks refuge in the almost inaccessible landscapes of Africa to leave us a moving testimony of humanity. Others discover how to weather the tempest with ability and grace, like P.G. Wodehouse, and prosper. Nothing is new under the sun; for more than two millennia originality and individuality are considered sins which the owners of the flock ineffectively try to eradicate. During the Twentieth Century success has come to be a necessity without which art losses meaning for the majority of the public, but true artists should labor only for those who are able to understand. The other option is to sacrifice the work for the sake of success, which in a short time will disappear just like any other out of fashion object. In the course of the last one hundred years it is not in music where the dissonant voices are heard most often, nor in the visual arts with its opportunistic protests of the past. Today a work of art – within the discipline of the plastic arts – is not created in the studio of the artist, nor with the paintbrush of the painter or the chisel of the sculptor. It *occurs* in the galleries when the client pays for it, and above all it *happens* if it is successful at the auction houses. It transcends and receives true recognition with the auctioneer's voice and acquires intrinsic value with the strike of the hammer. The museums of contemporary art and the collectors do the rest. In stark contrast to the period most exposed to the domination of the masses and their apologists, individuals like Fellini, Ford, Kurosawa, Wells and other directors nurtured the imagination of contemporary man by intoning glorious hymns of freedom. It is curious this was happening precisely within the artistic discipline that is most dependent on the public. To those cineastes we owe in some measure the presence of this exhibition. Their generous disposition in favor of fundamental values inspires it. Without the experiences left by film in the Twentieth Century conscience, perhaps fashion along with special interests would have prevailed and the numbers would have ended up deciding in favor of the less substantial, but more familiar and productive. There isn't anything which deserves greater reward than that obtained by our discovery. We only aspire to fulfill an unavoidable commitment that exists within ourselves.

Modern painting and sculpture have been enriched by abstract concepts and materials and sometimes the significance has been overvalued. Some opportunists, ignoring the training and knowledge required for all creative work, have ventured with success in this arena by taking advantage of a confusing situation. The more capable artists, however, often maximize their talent and sensibility in applying the new ingredients. Romero strains to get a look at the twenty-first century crammed with considerable baggage of past aesthetic culture. The work he realizes is nurtured by his knowledge of Renaissance painters and classical sculptors; he has managed to understand them through a profound study of what they have realized. Sustained by this understanding he is able to contemplate his surroundings in a world that every day becomes smaller and closer to him. From the country where he lives, he manages to understand each of the artistic movements that have surged forth during the past century and while interested in them, he remains faithful to his personal iconography and style. He grew up surrounded by the pictorial realism that is Mexico, in touch with abstract art and not far from the American vanguard movements. He respects and admires the forerunners of these schools, without being seduced by any of them. As Spinoza informs us, life in its innumerable manifestations is part of nature; feeling and memory are the only things that die and everything else is transformed. Also, art is one, although with multiple variations and incalculable possibilities of expression. An artist not only needs to have ideas, but at the core must possess a sensibility that will enable him to communicate with the public. Romero knows this and possibly for this reason opens his intuition to everything that surges around him. He is delighted by the novels of Ibarguengoitia and Rulfo, as well as Hemingway and Faulkner and dives into the essays of Umberto Eco. His curiosity is unrestrained and it is possibly due to this condition that the work he realizes is comprehensible and sophisticated at the same time, within reach of average people with awareness or a more cosmopolitan public. To view what he does gives the spectator the impression of being in the presence of a mind both original and deep. It is stimulating for me to discover that within this universal language there may still be an extensive field within figurative art yet to be explored.

J.M. TASENDE

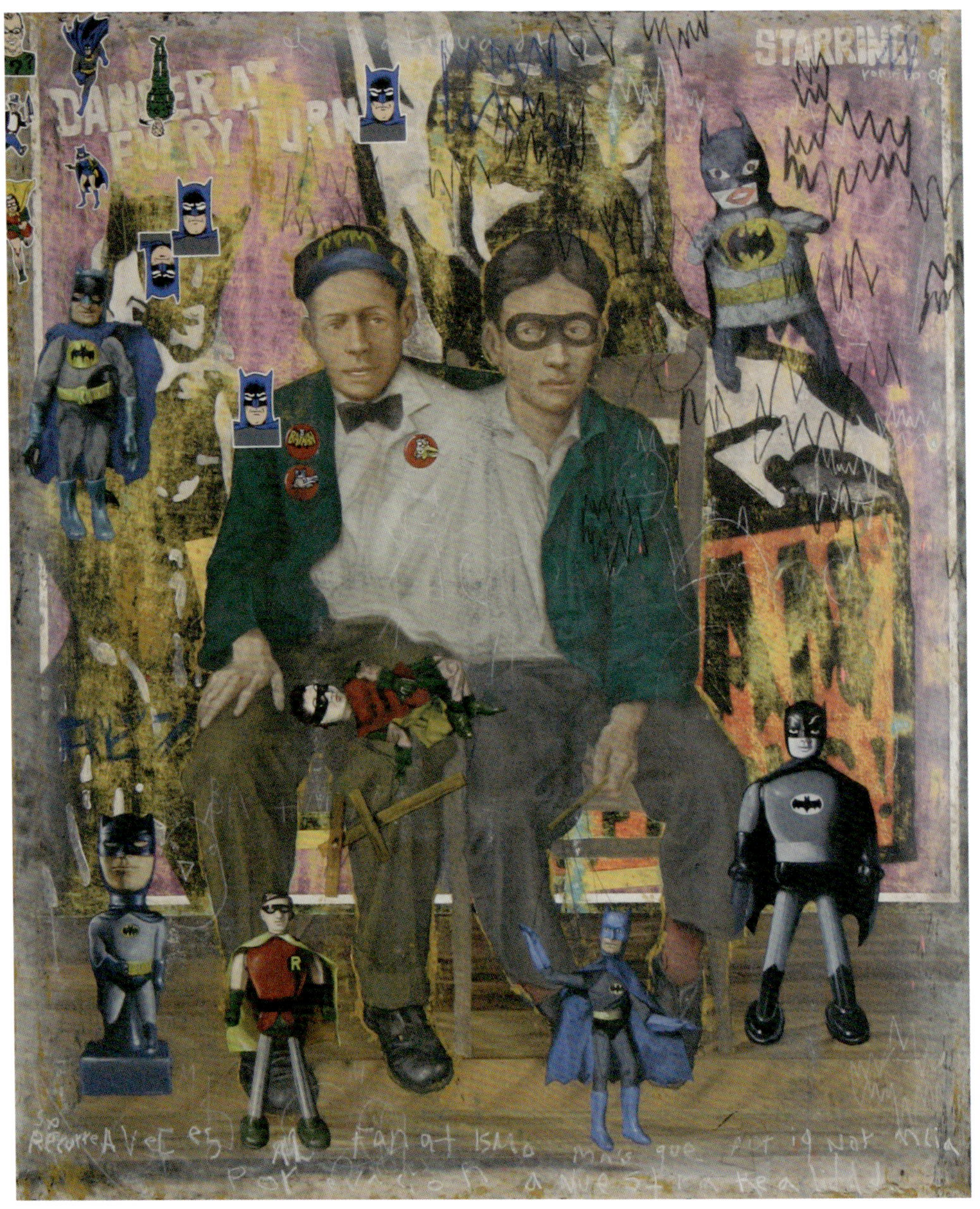

5 **Siamese Twins** 2008
Oil on canvas
47 x 39 ¼ inches

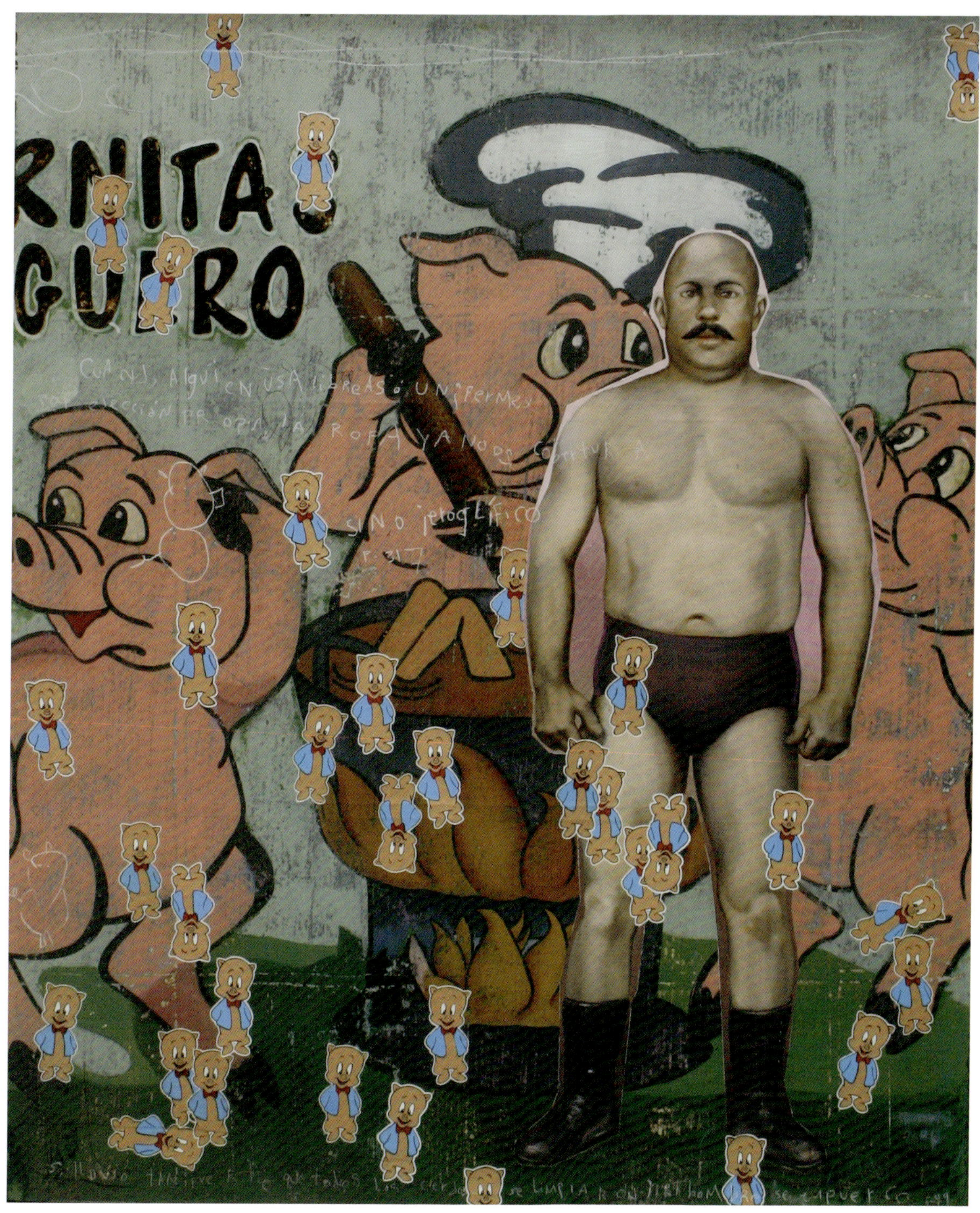

6 Pork Flakes (The Gladiator) 2006
Oil on canvas
71 x 59 inches

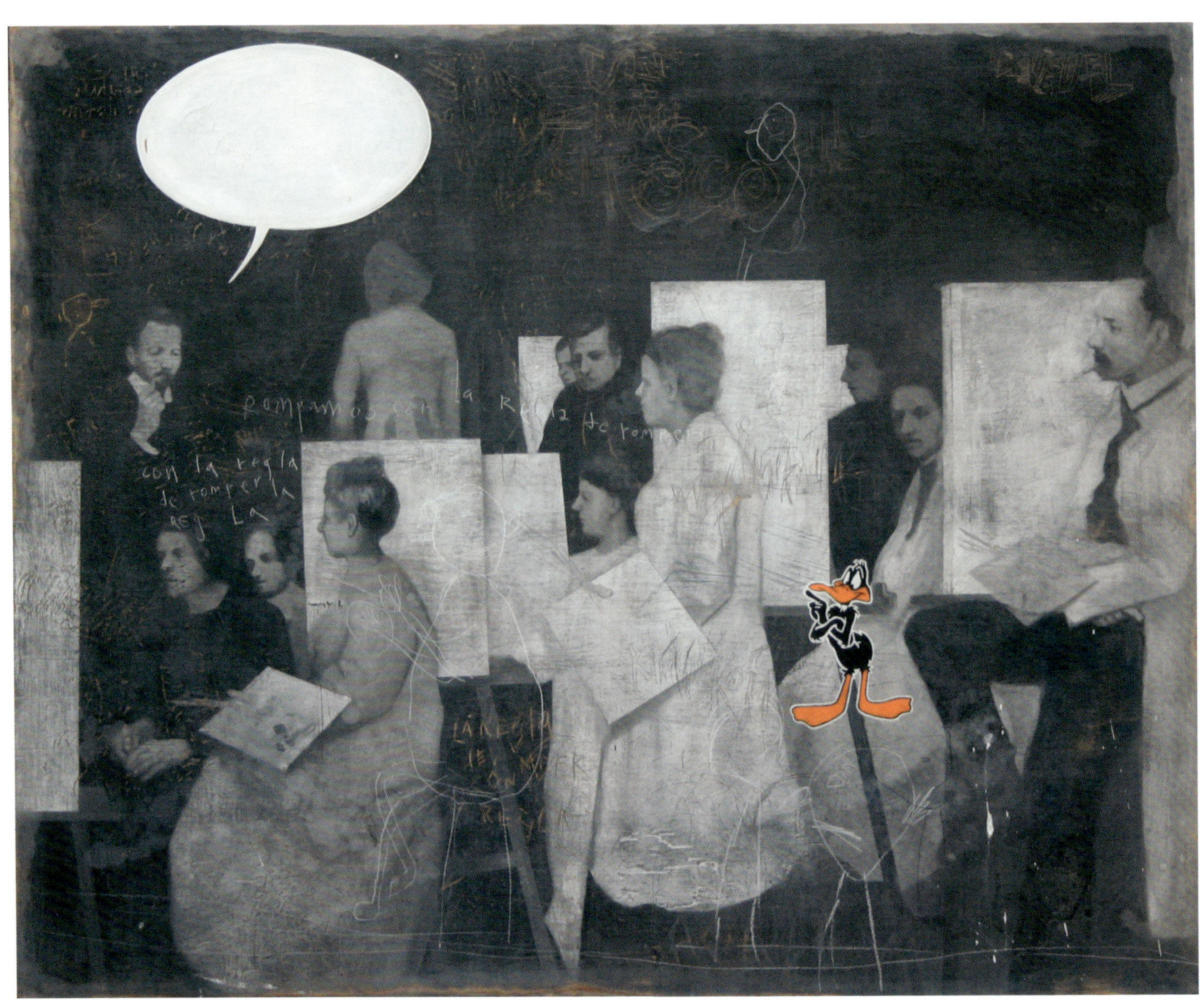

7 **Drawing Classes** 2008
Oil on wood panel
47 ¼ x 59 inches

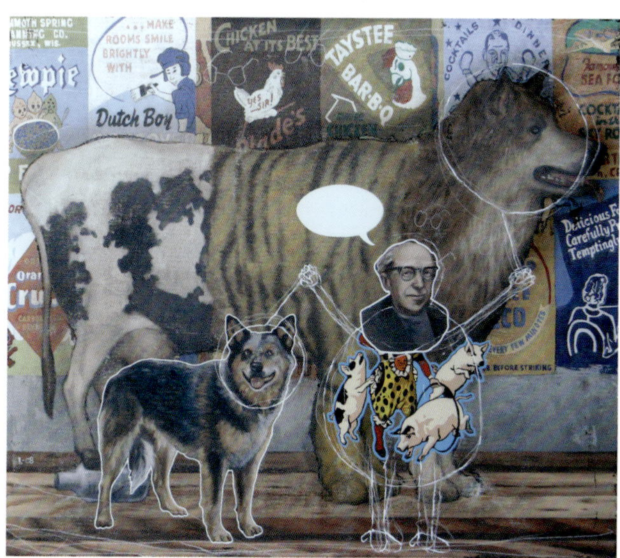

8 **Amazing Animal 2** 2008
Oil on canvas
26 x 30 inches

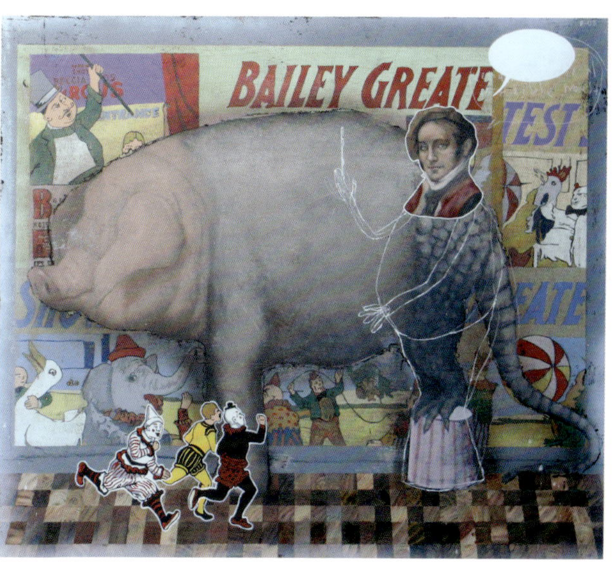

9 **Amazing Animal 3** 2008
Oil on canvas
26 x 30 inches

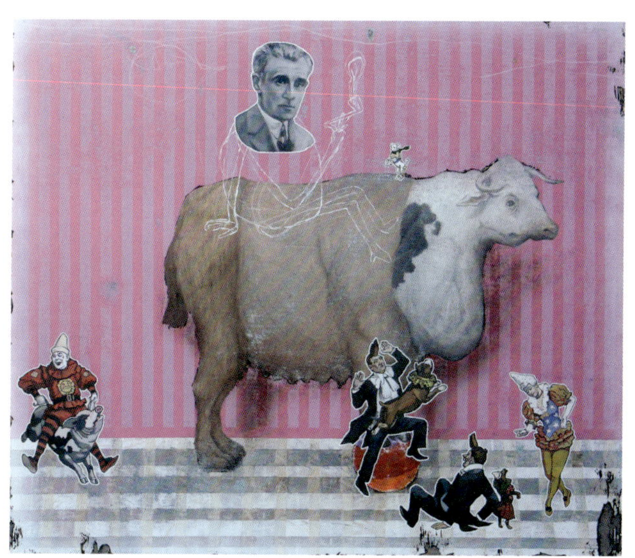

10 **Amazing Animal 4** 2008
Oil on canvas
26 x 30 inches

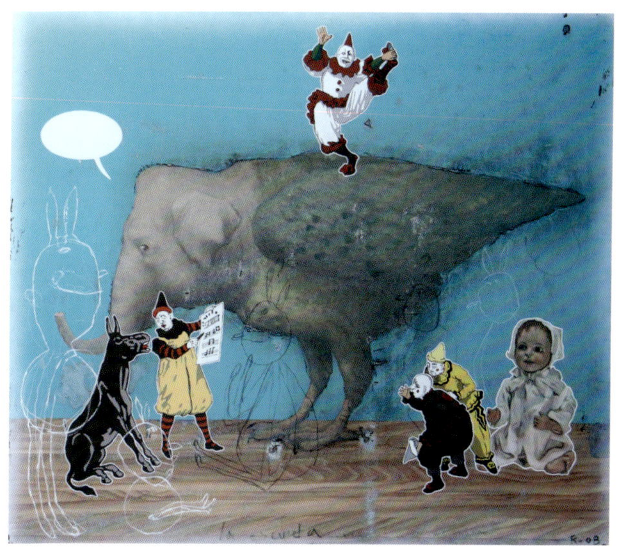

11 **Amazing Animal 7** 2008
Oil on canvas
26 x 30 inches

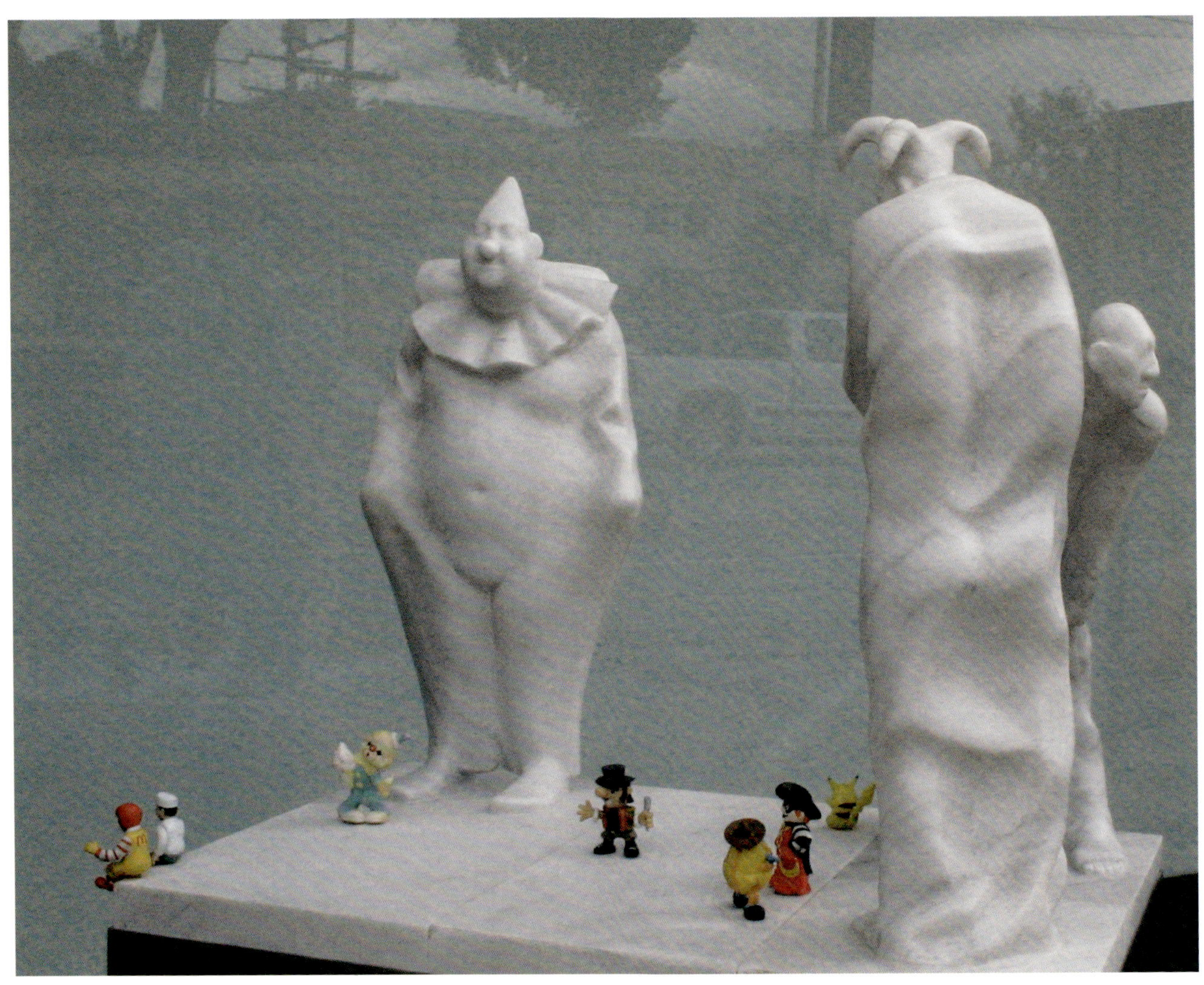

12 **The Circus** 2007
Marble, unique
21 x 18 x 23 ¾ inches

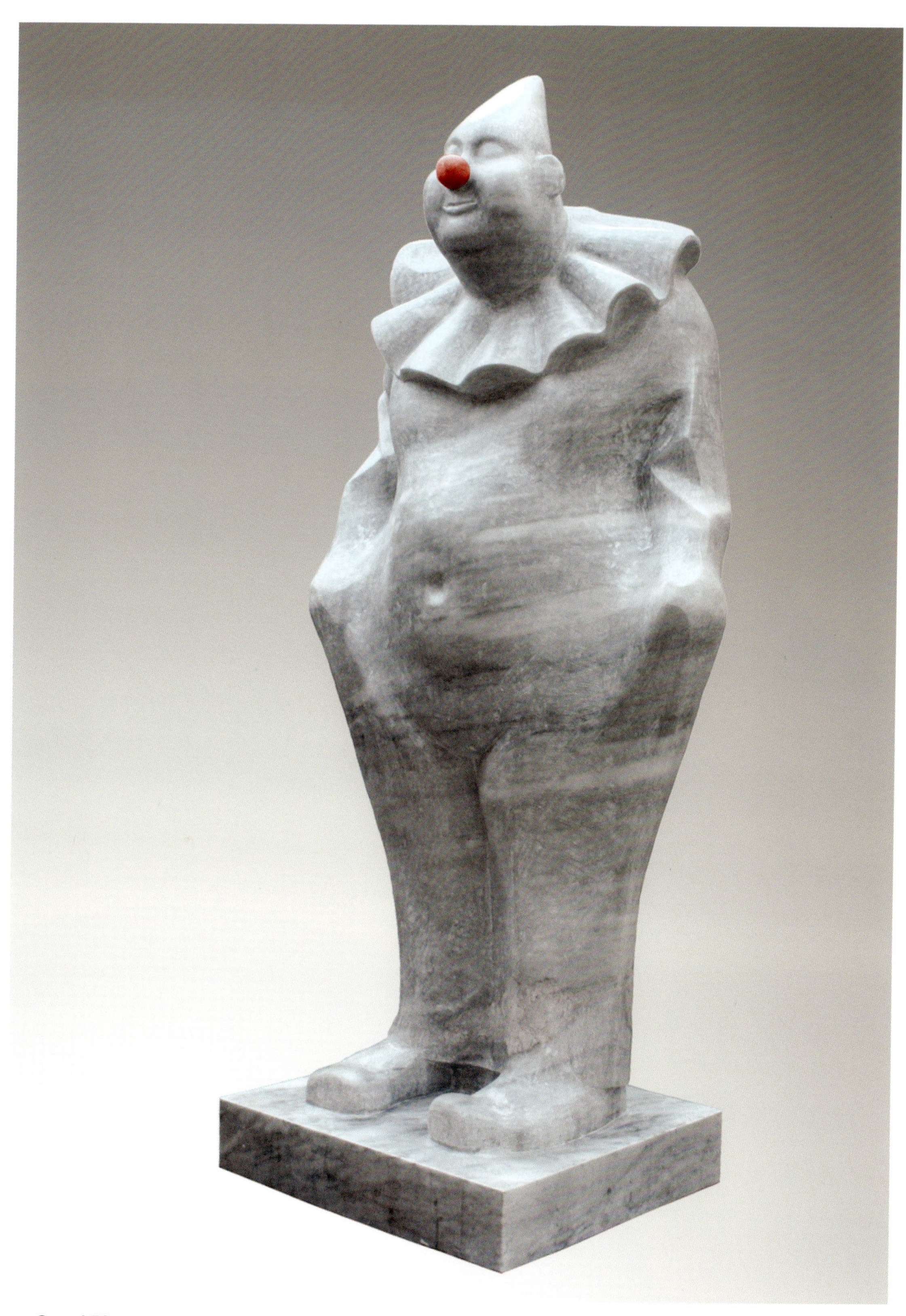

16 **Grand Pierrot** 2008
Marble, unique
72 inches tall

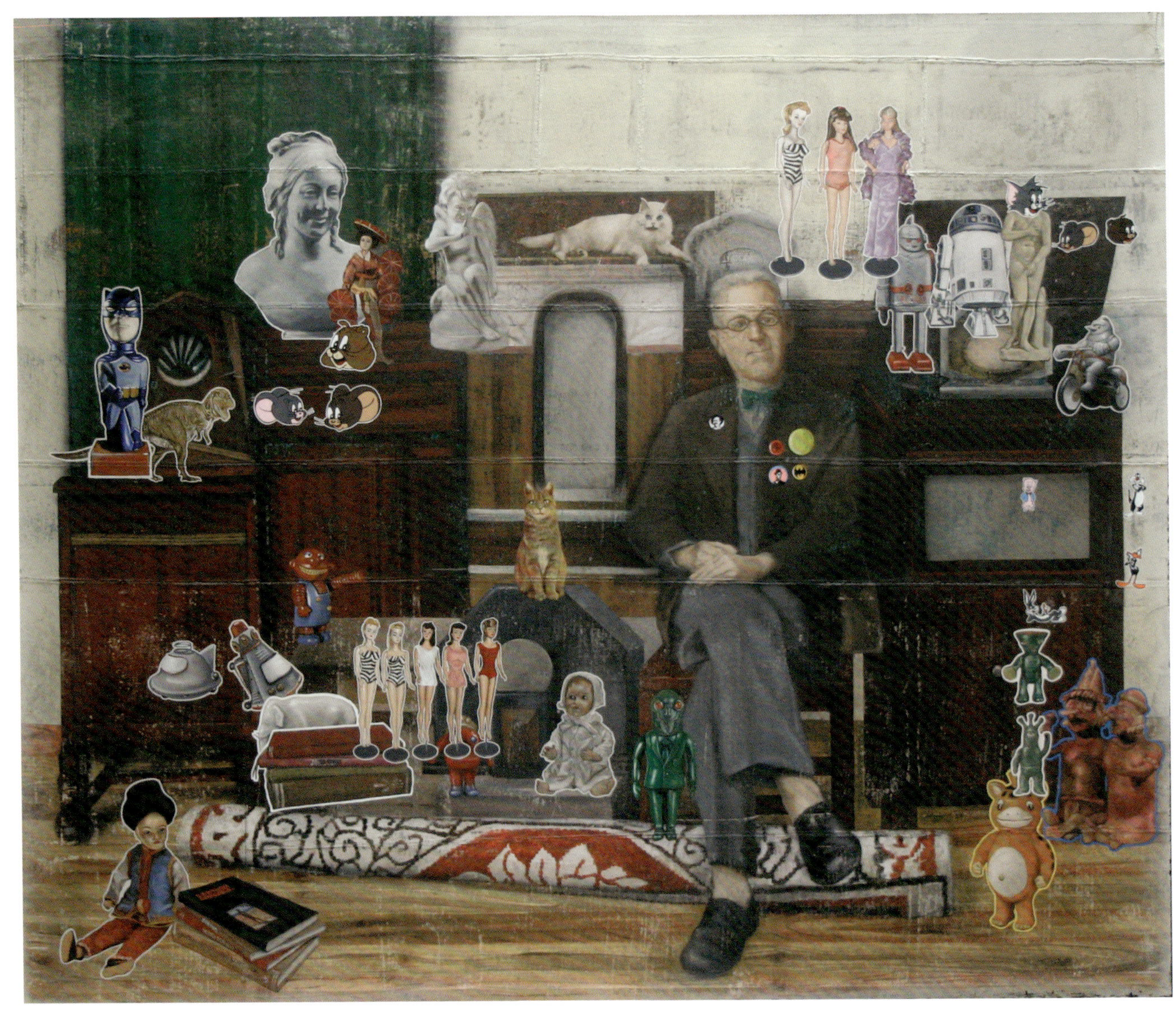

17 The Collector 2007
Oil on canvas
51 x 70 ¾ inches

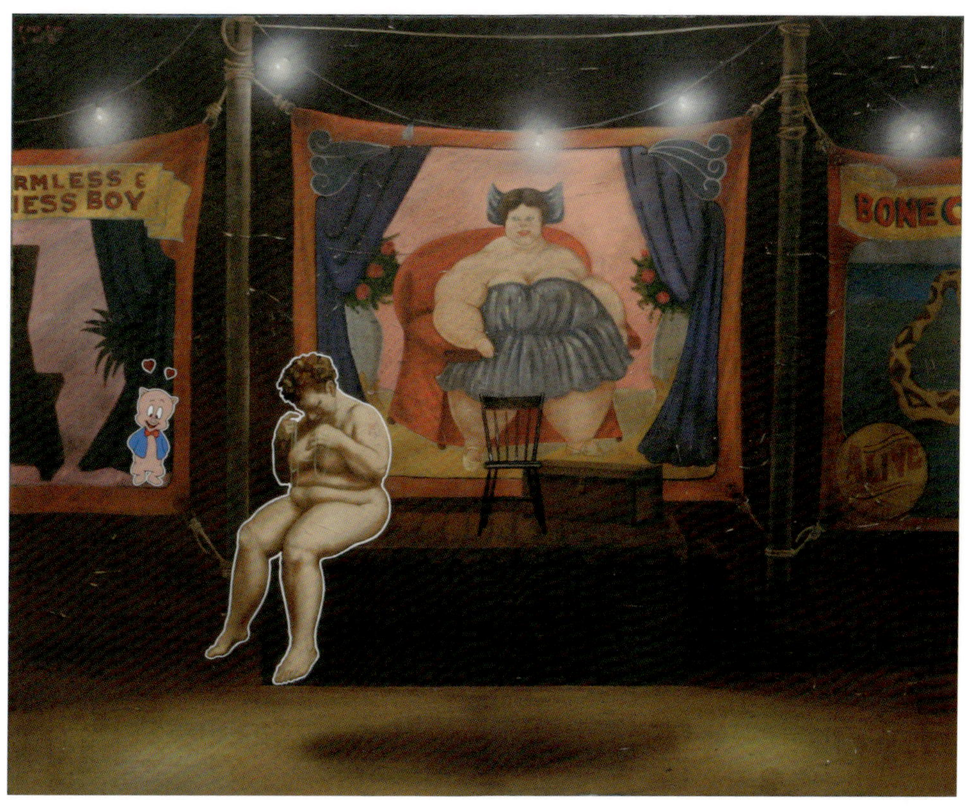

18 **Interior** 2008
Oil on wood panel
47 ¼ x 59 inches

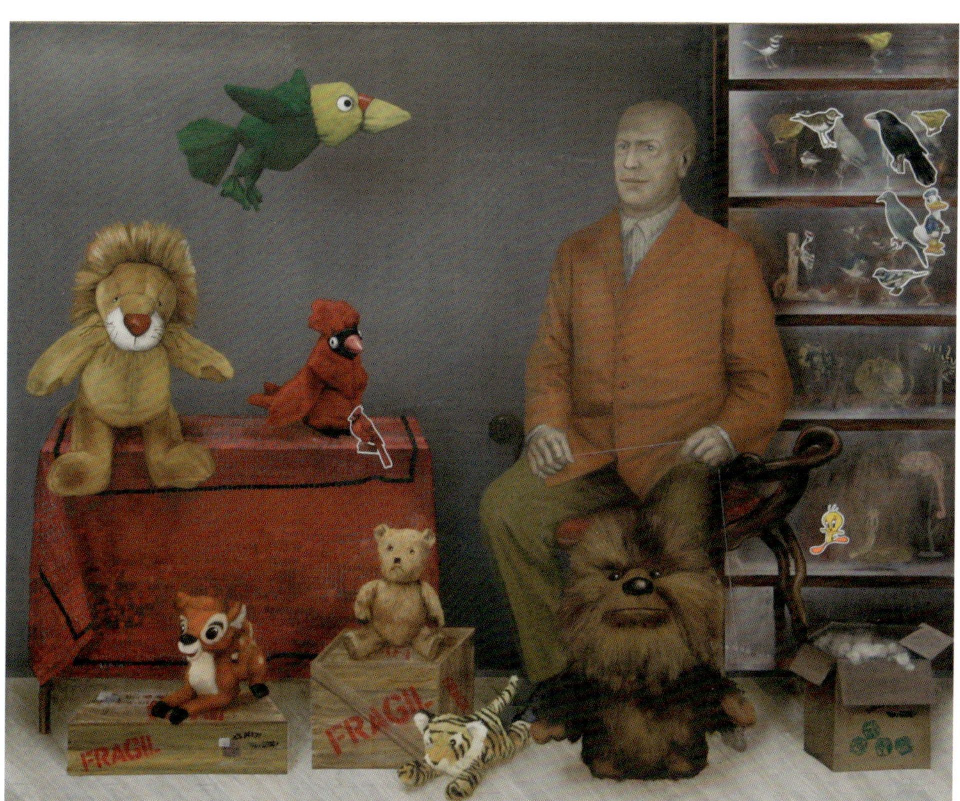

19 **Taxidermist** 2008
Oil on wood panel
47 ¼ x 59 inches

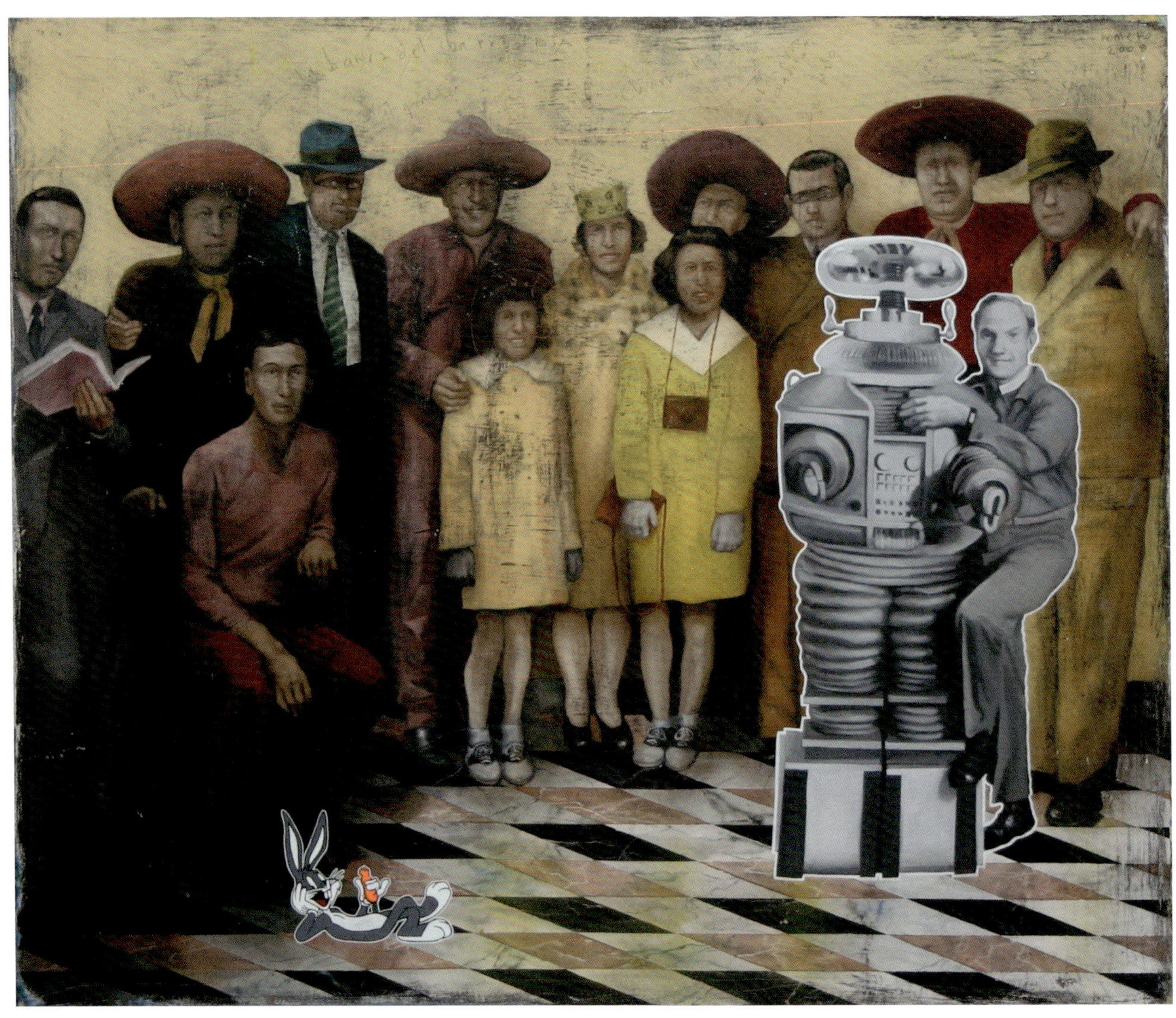

20 **Estudios Churubusco** 2008
Oil on wood panel
39 3/8 x 47 ¼ inches

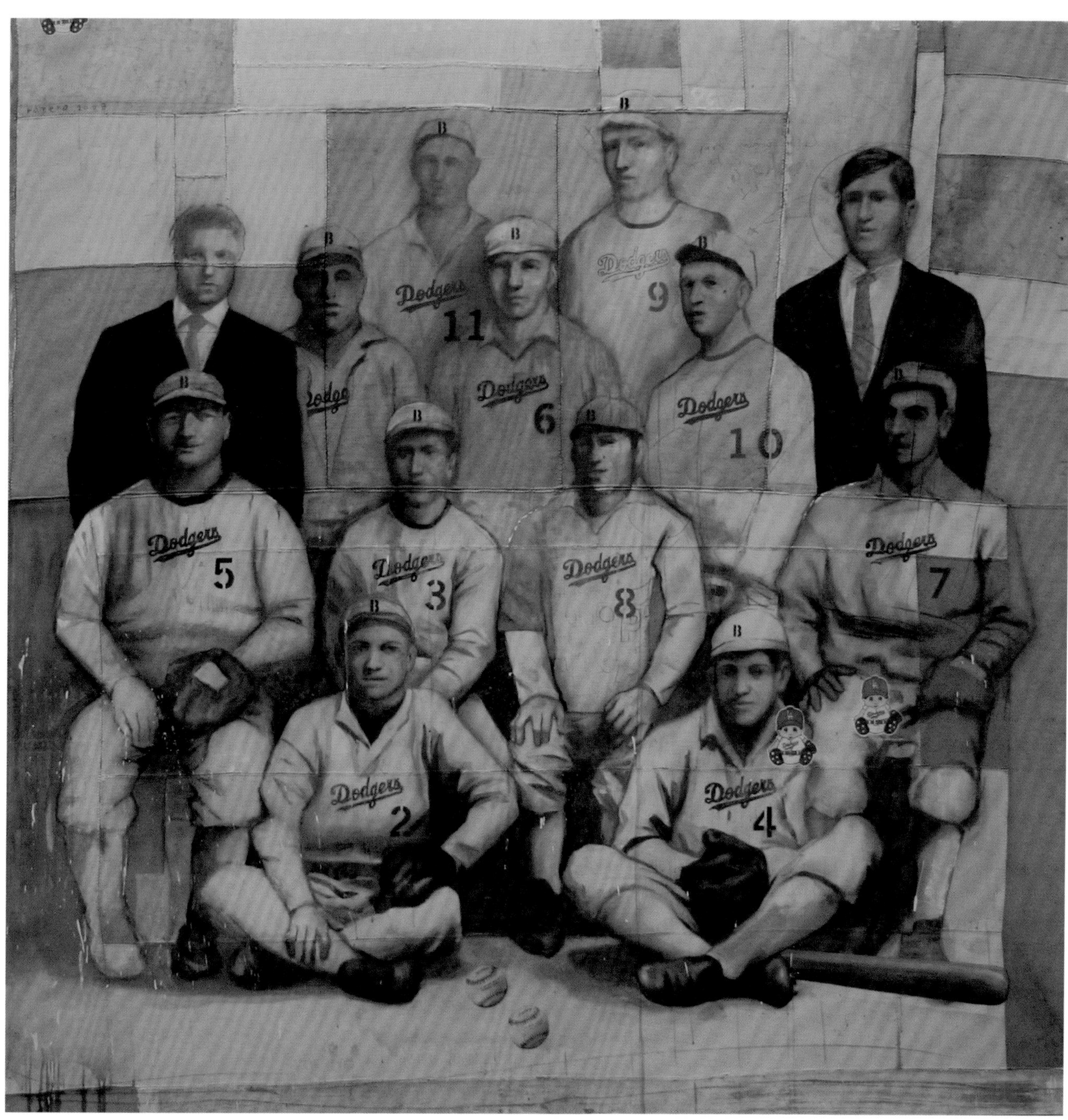

21 **Dodgers** 2008
Oil on canvas
78 ¾ x 78 ¾ inches

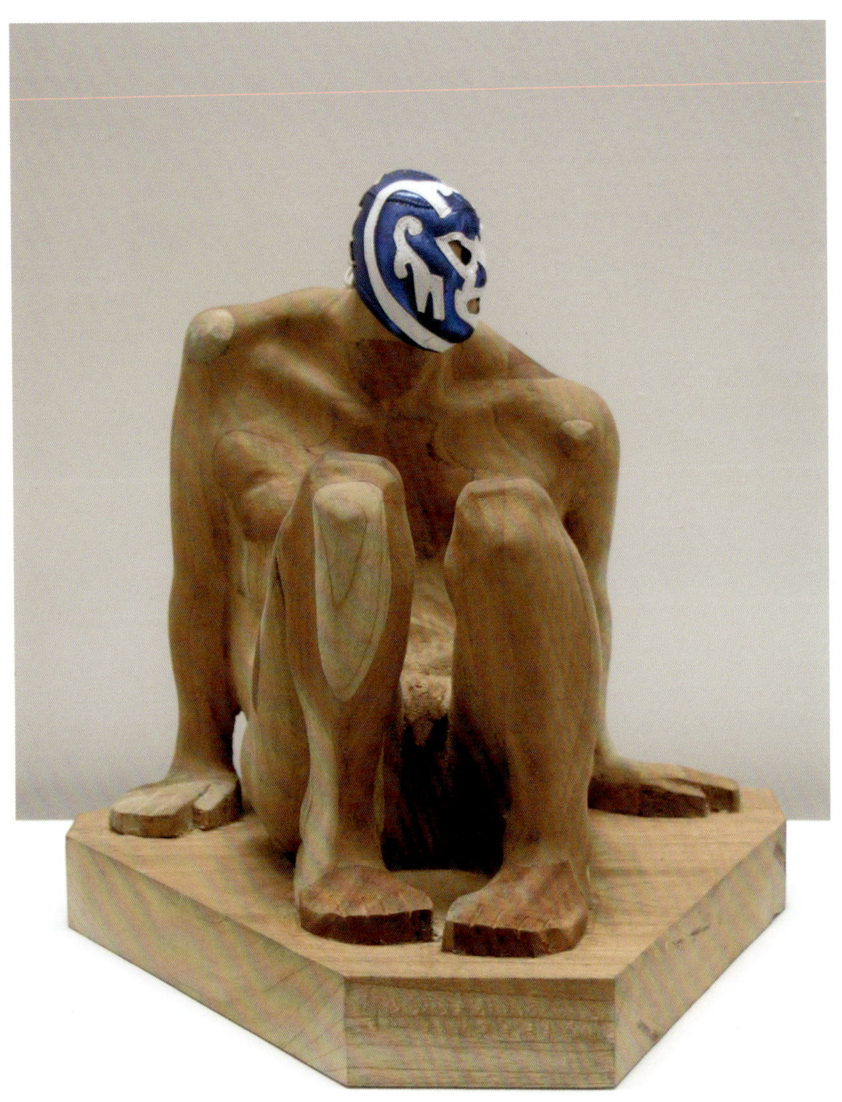

22 **Seated Pride** 2008
Wood and vinyl, unique
15 ¾ x 16 x 15 ½ inches

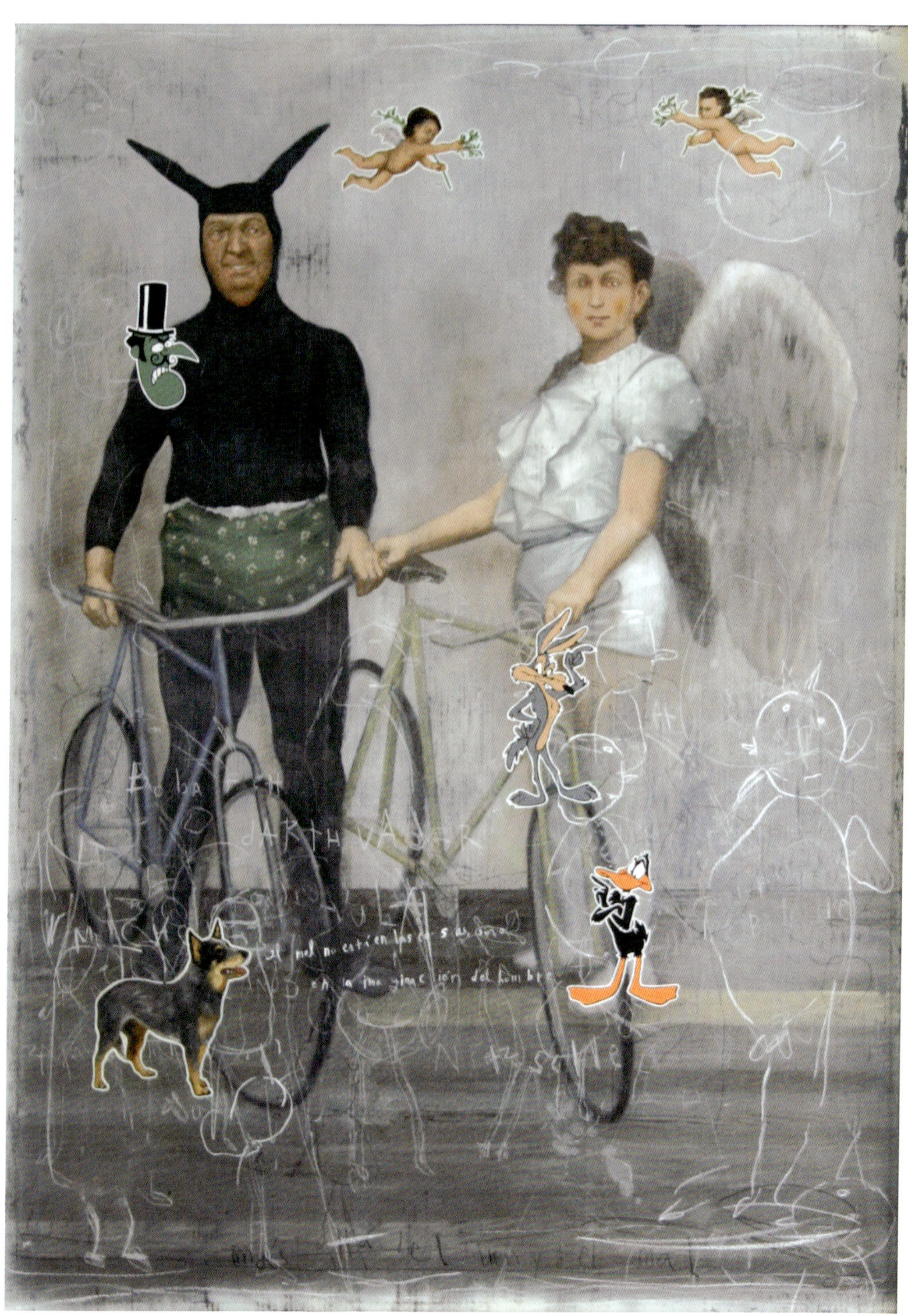

24 **Beyond Good and Evil** 2007
Oil on canvas
55 x 39 ½ inches

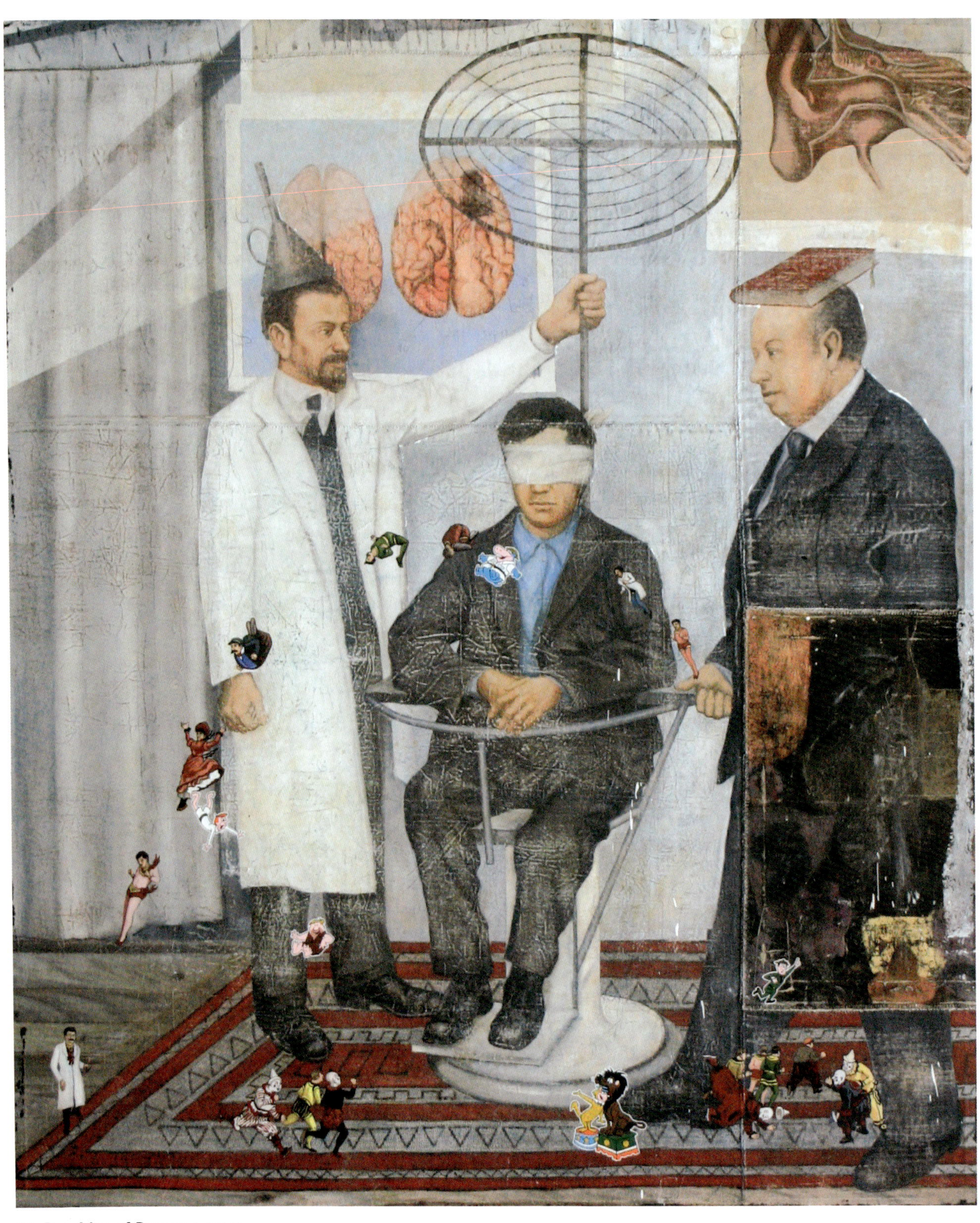

25 **Provider of Dreams** 2007
Oil on canvas
70 ¾ x 55 inches

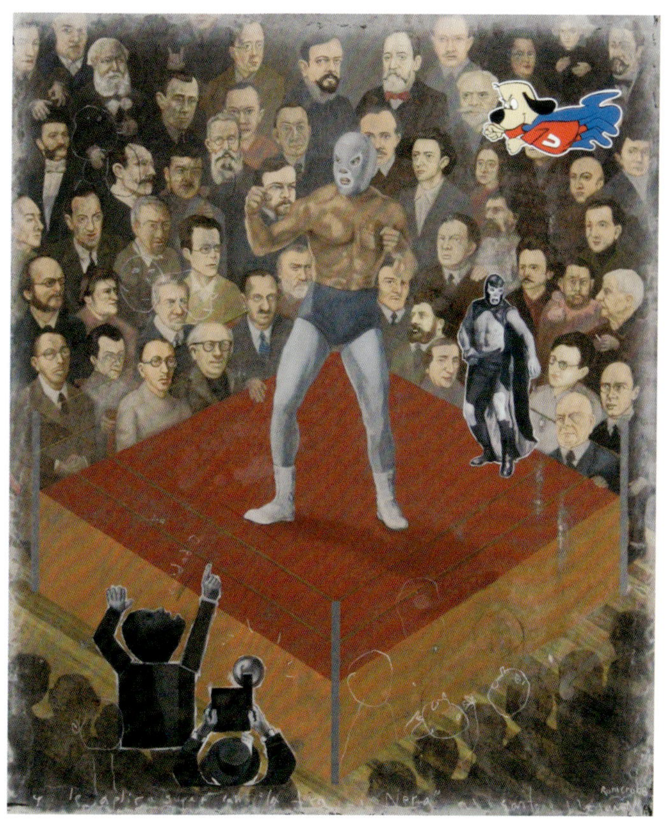

26 **Personajes Históricos** 2008
Oil on canvas
47 x 39 ¼ inches

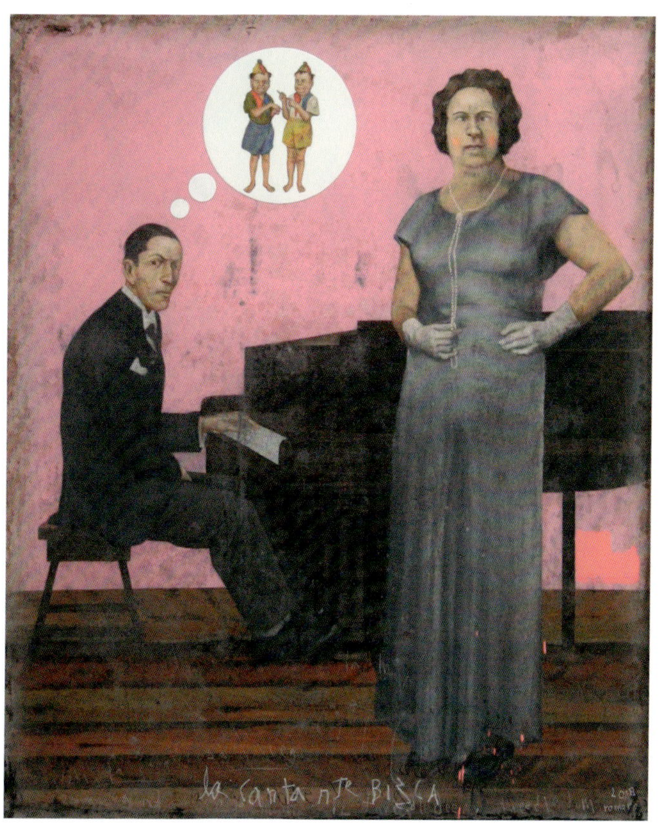

27 **Vende Caro Tu Amor** 2008
Oil on canvas
47 x 39 ¼ inches

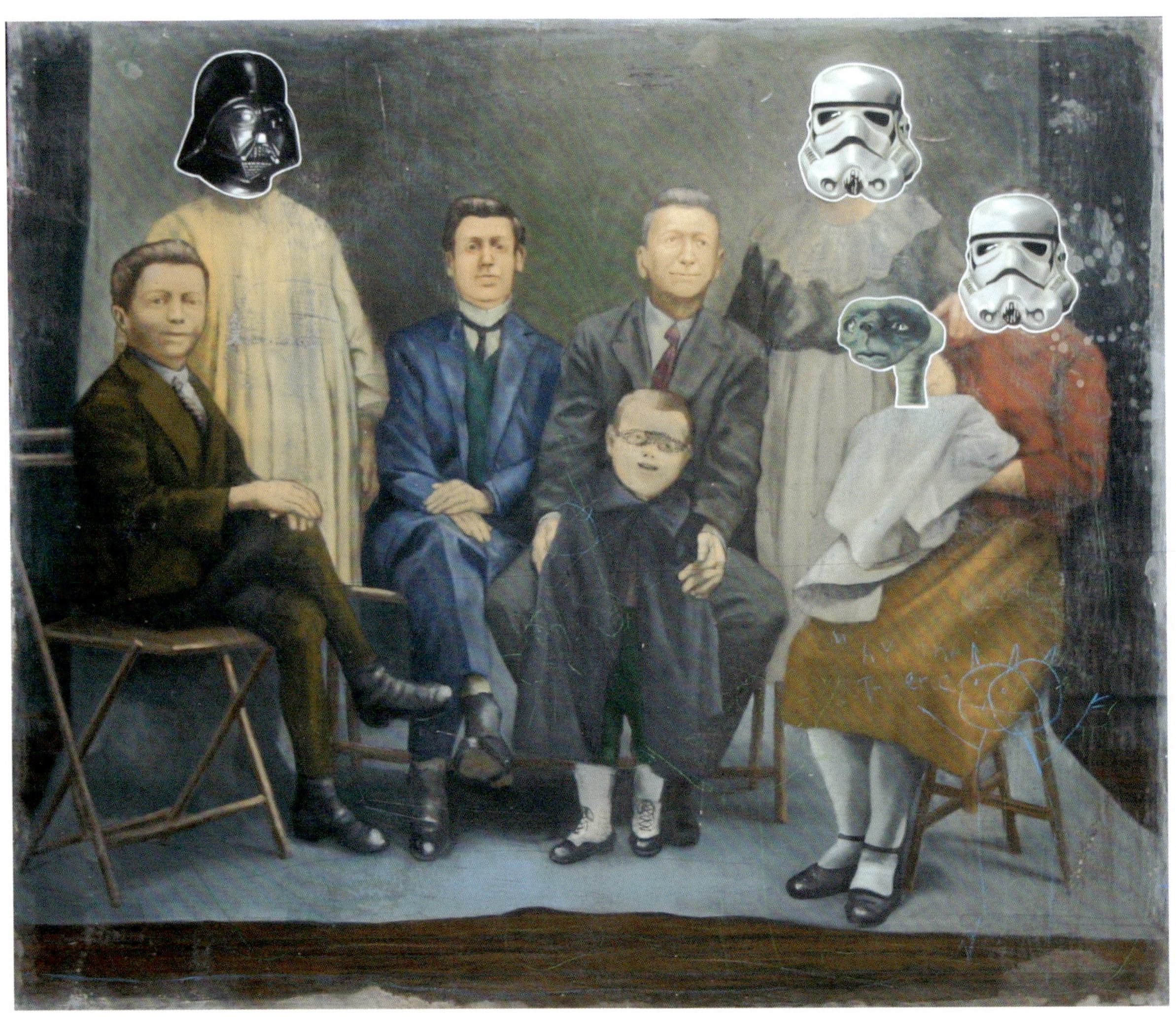

28 **Star Wars** 2008
Oil on wood panel
39 3/8 x 47 ¼ inches

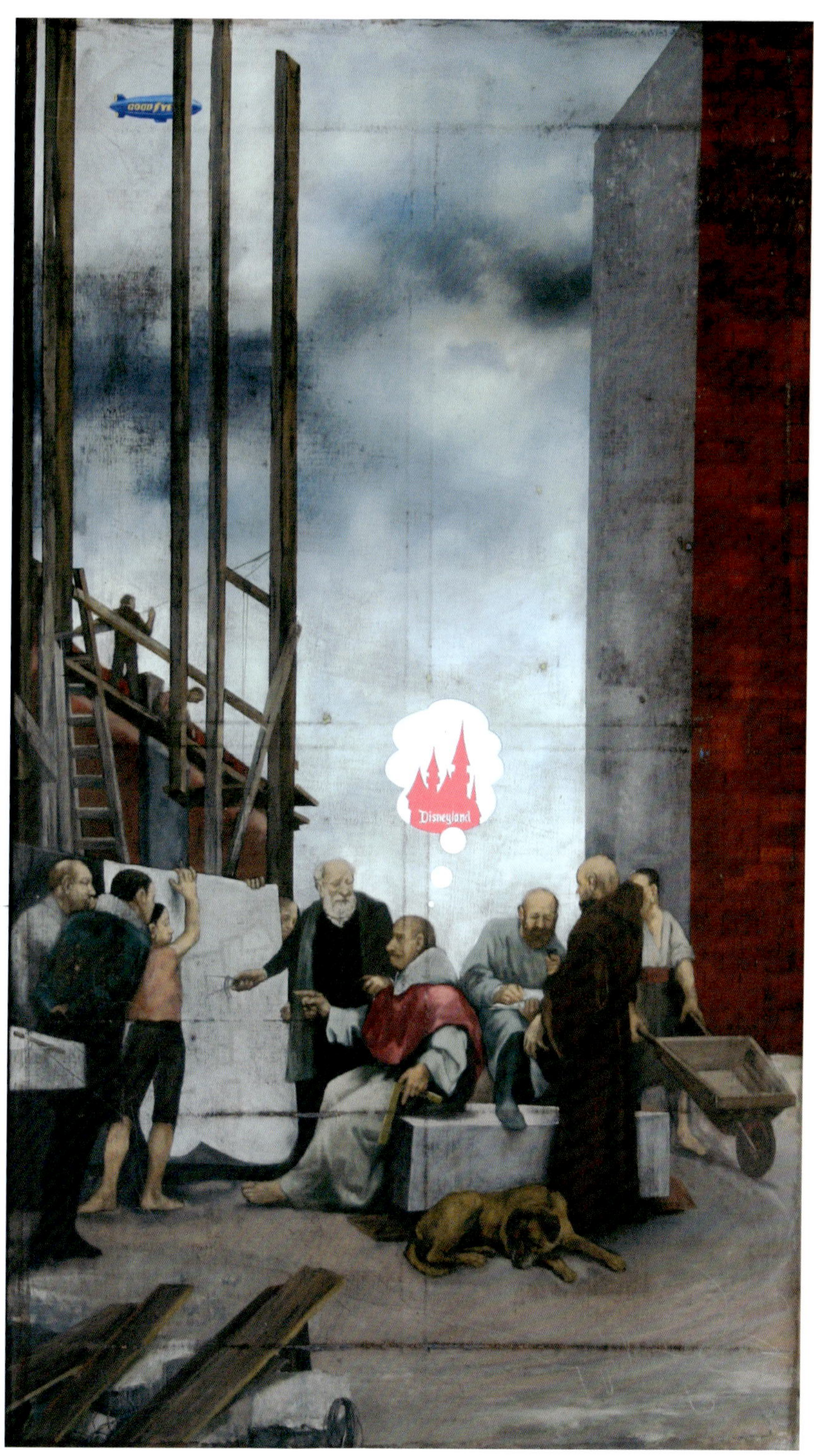

30 Futuristic Architects 2008
Oil on canvas
55 1/8 x 31 ½ inches

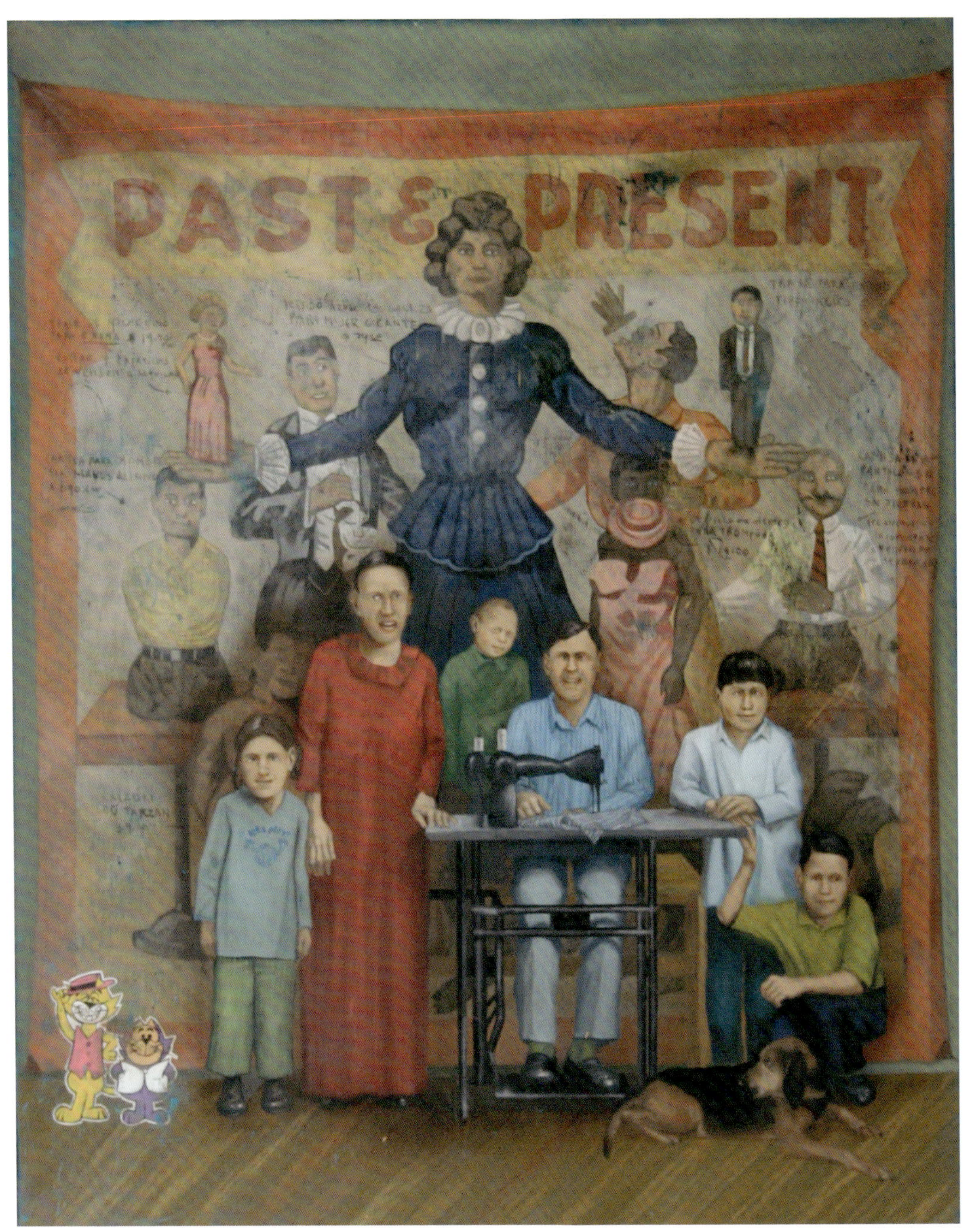

31 **Tailor to the Freaks** 2008
Oil on wood panel
59 ¼ x 47 ¼ inches

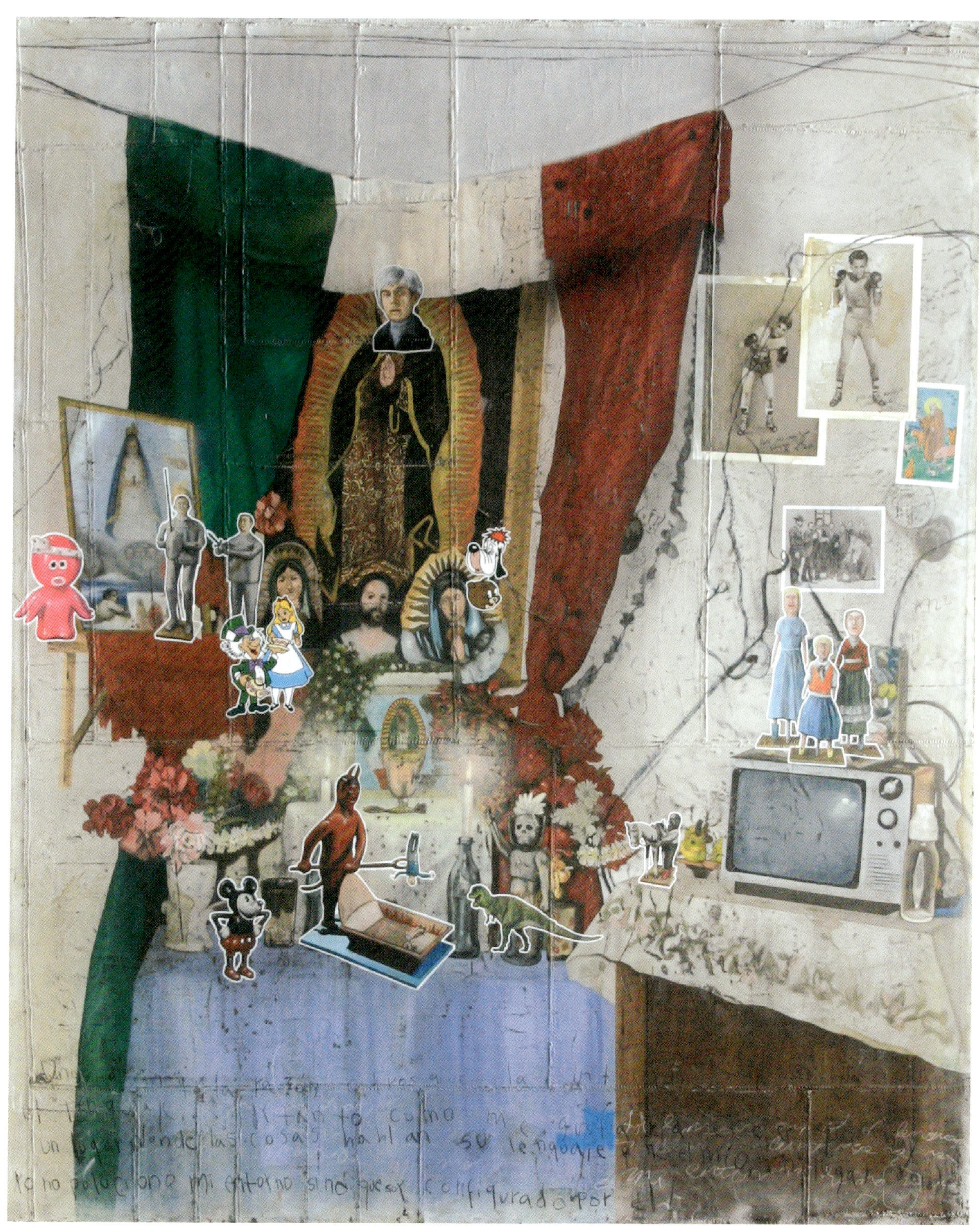

32 Echo Park 2008
Oil on canvas
74 ½ x 62 ¾ inches

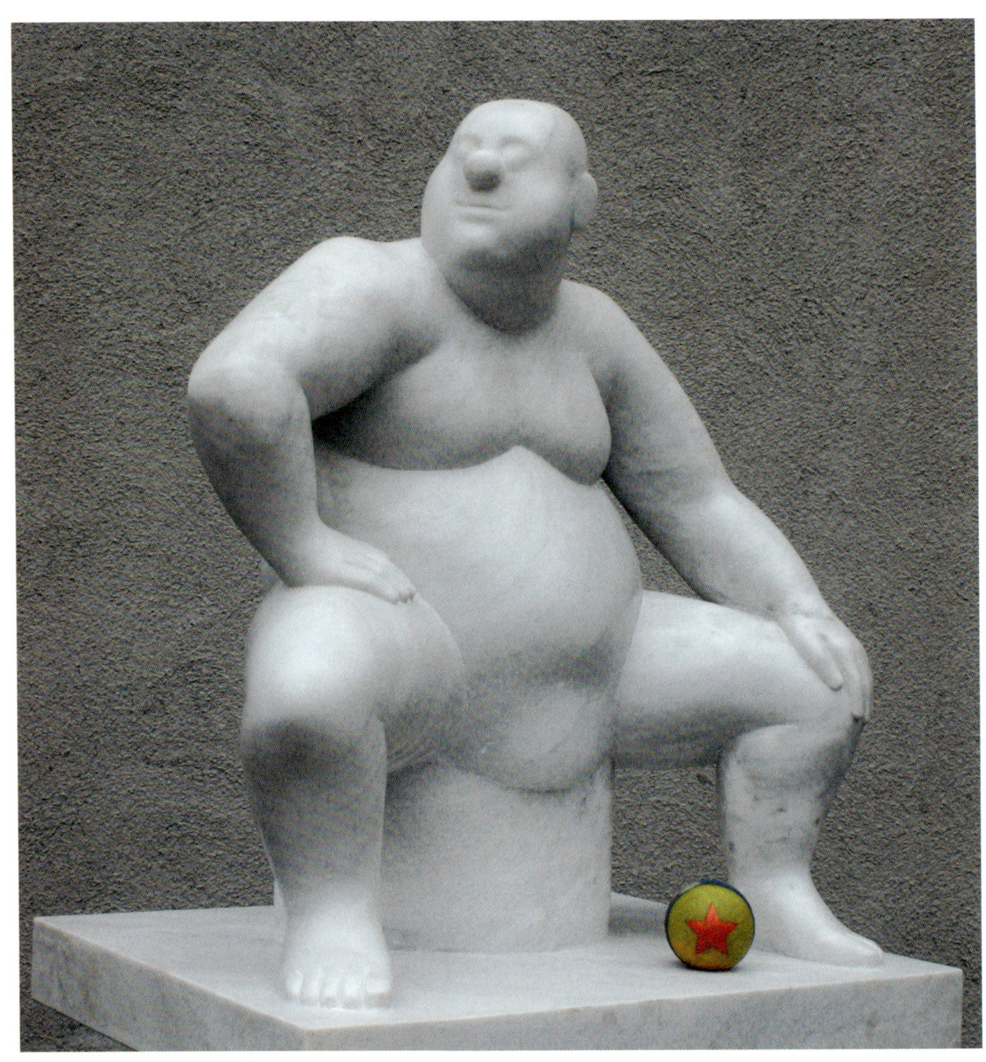

33 **Thinking of a New Joke** 2007
Marble, unique
26 ¾ x 21 ¾ x 17 inches

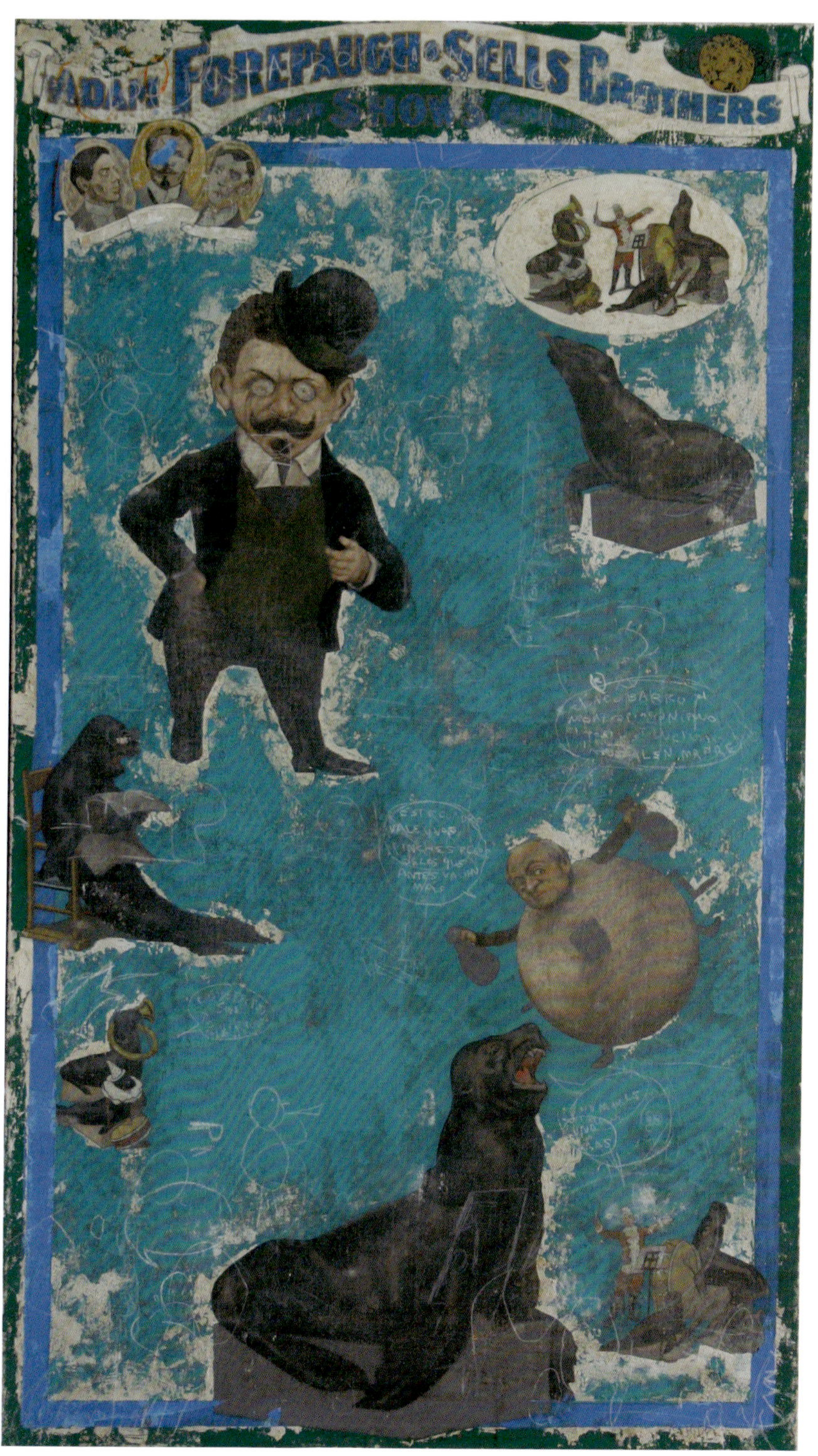

35 Three Ring Circus 1991
Oil on canvas
59 x 34 ½ inches

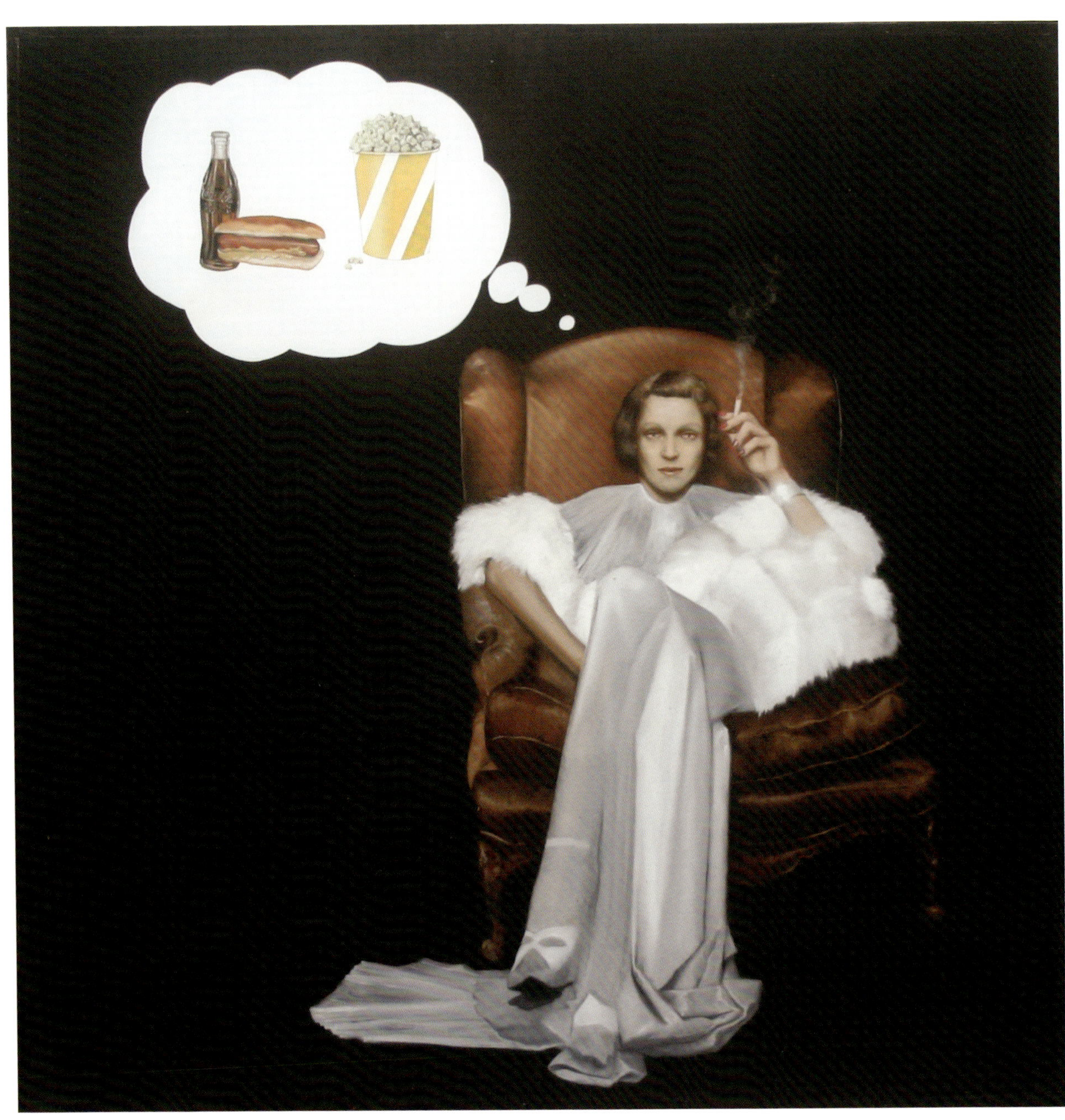

36 **Marlene** 2008
Oil on canvas
78 ¾ x 78 ¾ inches

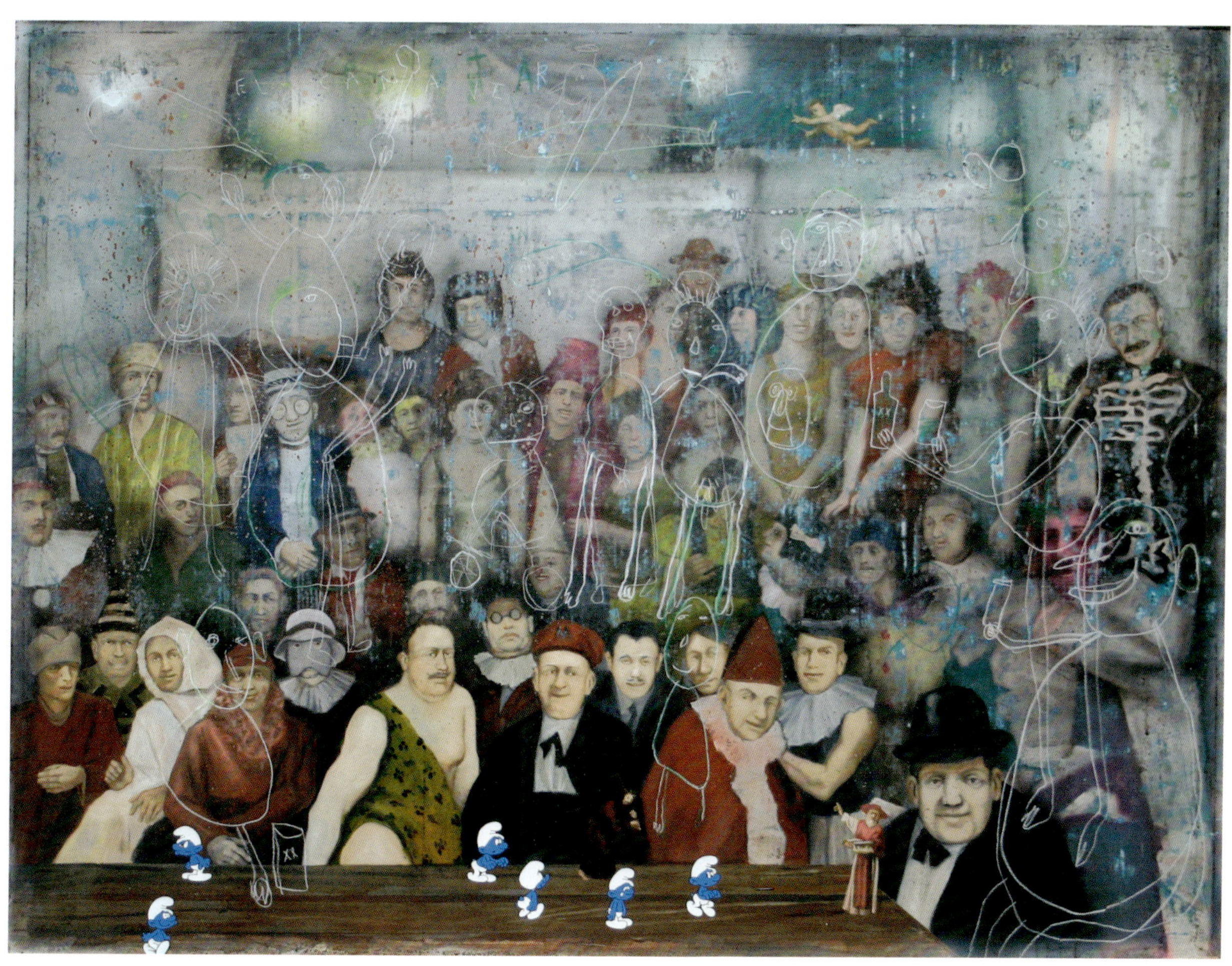

37 **Familiar Faces** 2008
Oil on canvas
59 1/8 x 78 ¾ inches

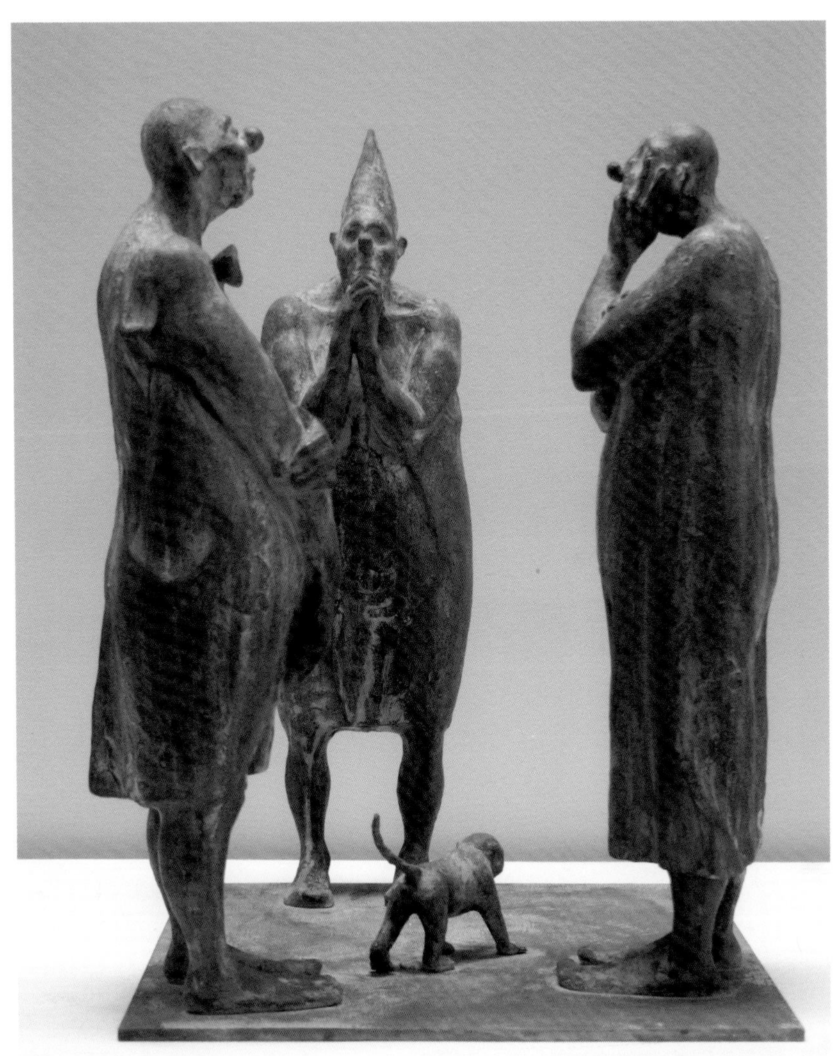

38 **Coloquio** 2008
Bronze, unique
19 ¼ x 17 x 14 inches

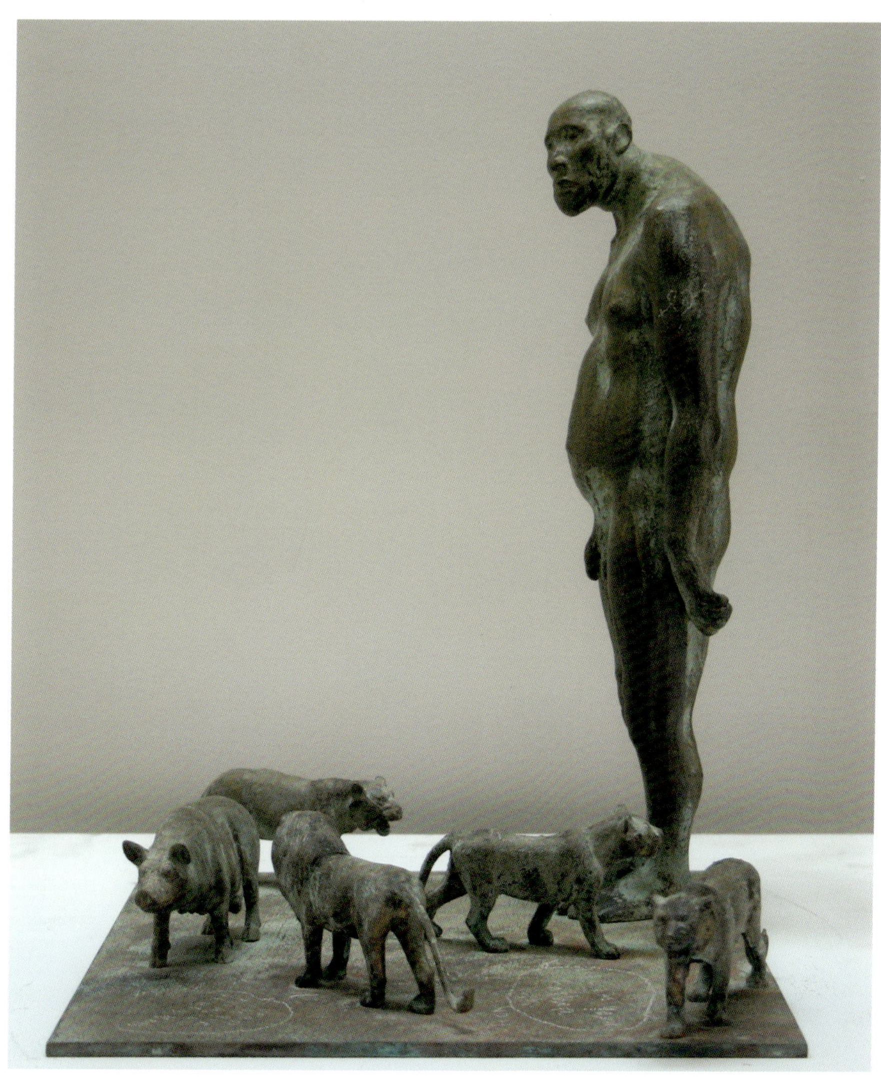

39 **The Giant** 2008
Bronze, unique
18 ¼ x 16 ½ x 14 1/8 inches

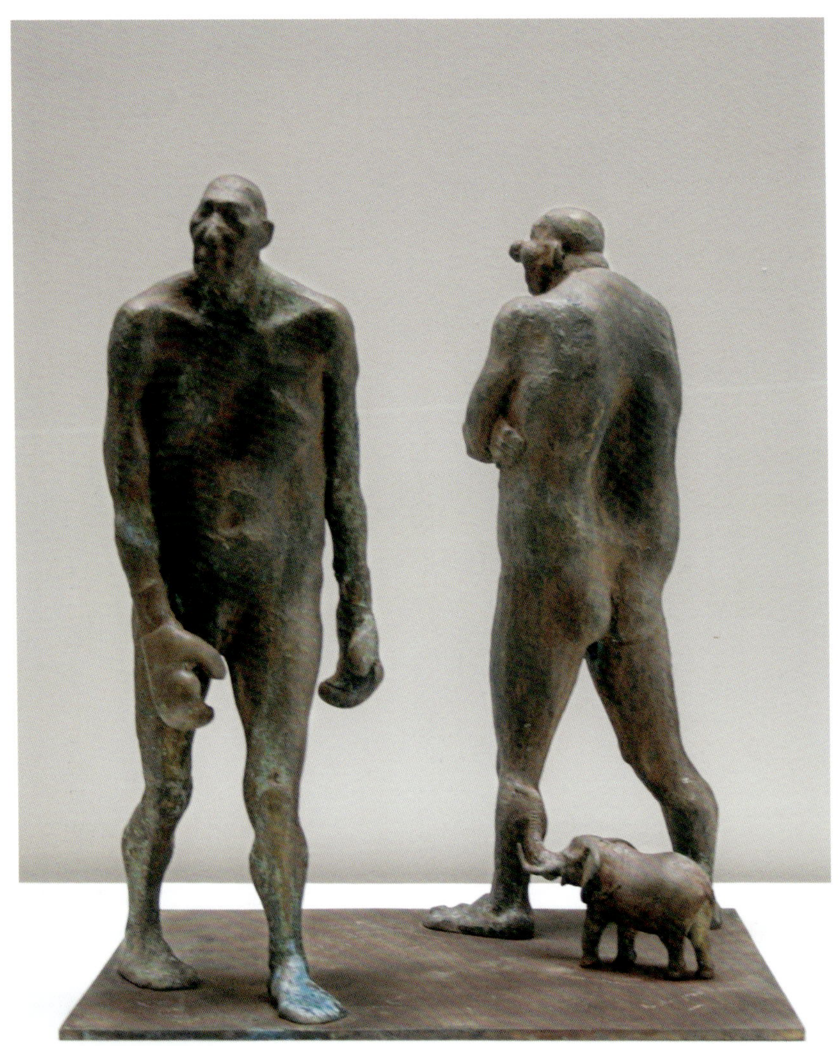

40 **The Elephant** 2008
Bronze, unique
18 x 15 ¾ x 14 ½ inches

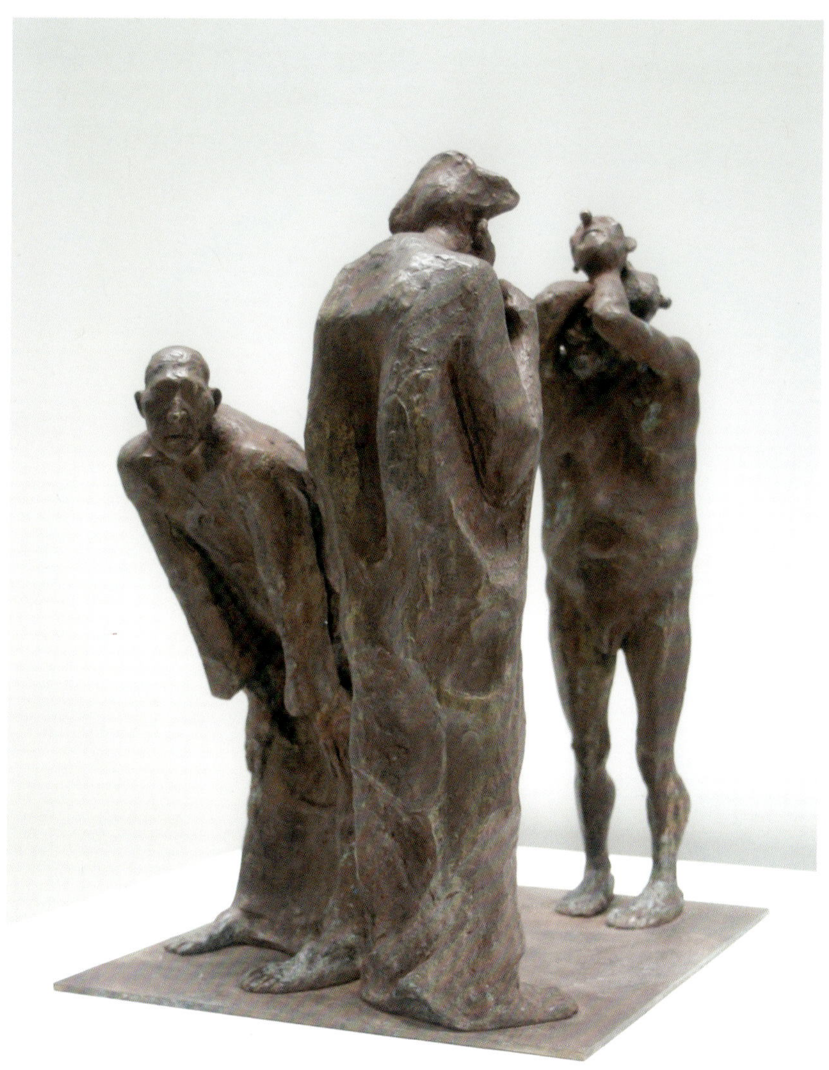

41 **Clowns** 2008
Bronze, unique
19 ¾ x 16 ½ x 13 ¾ inches

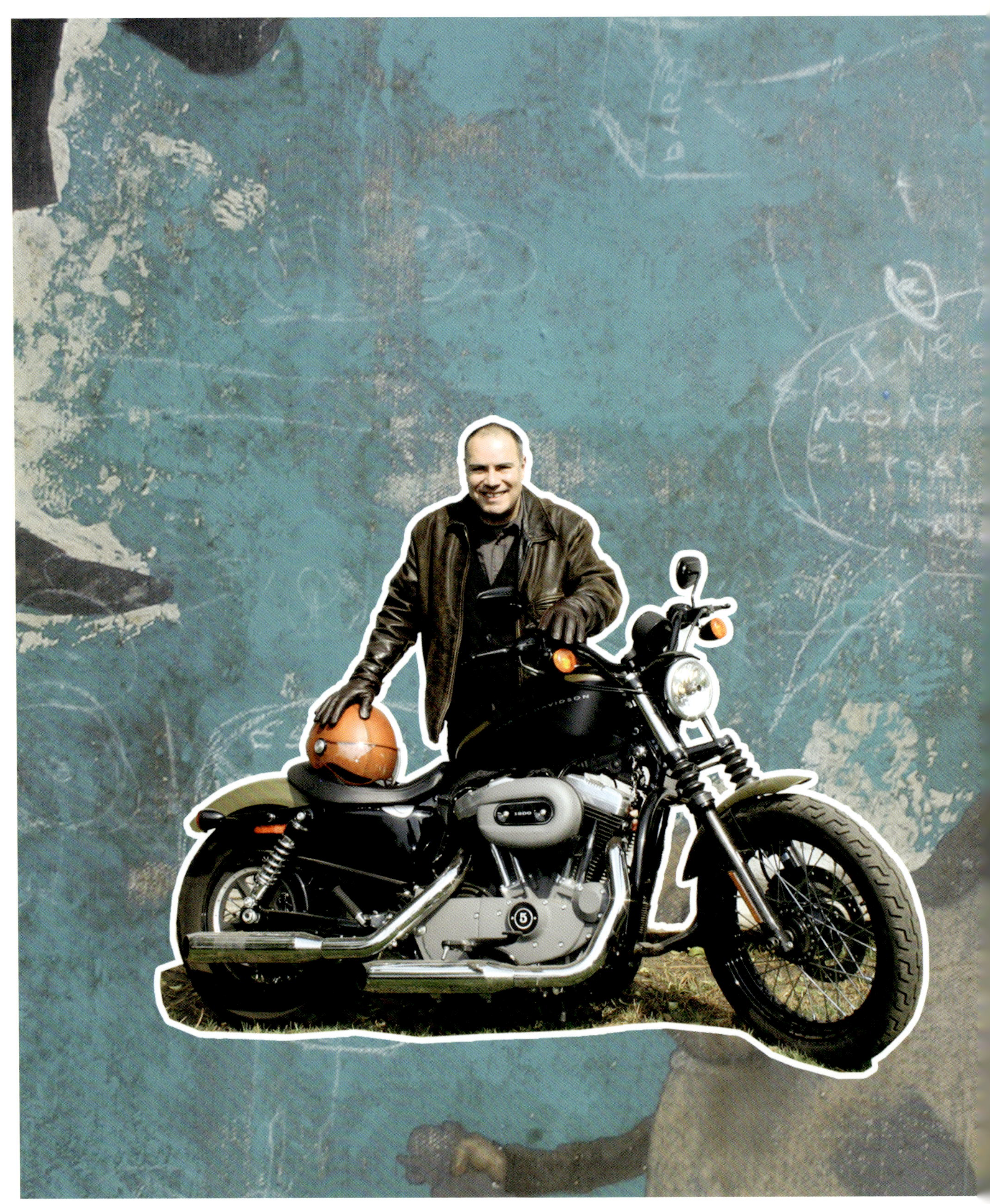

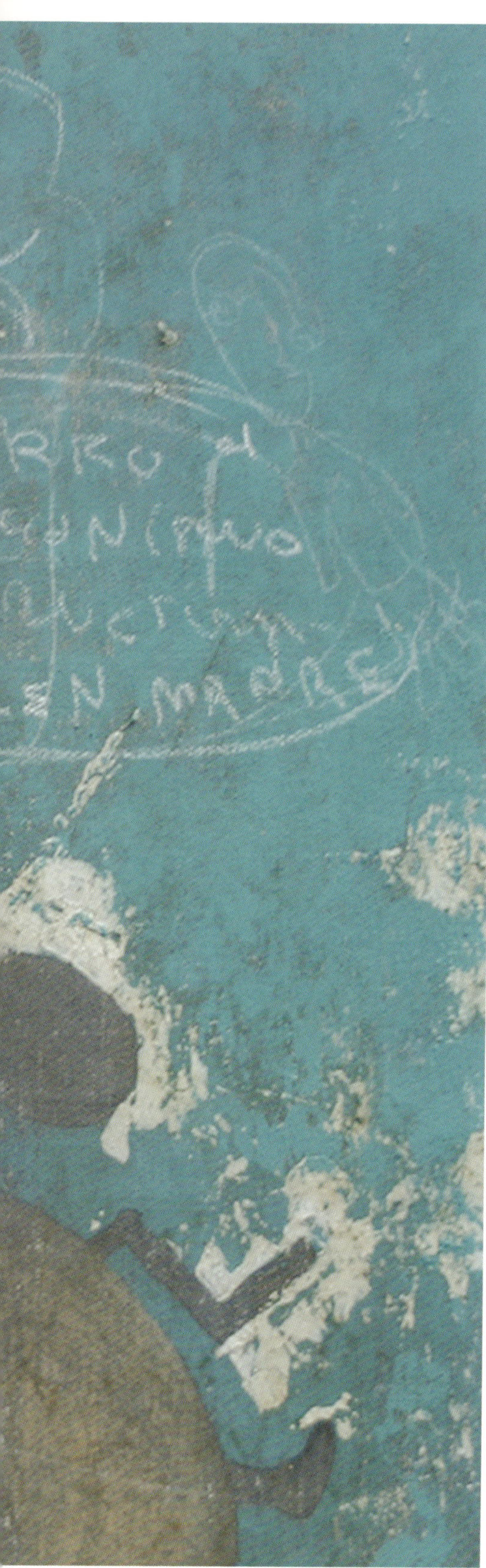

Armando Romero, Mexico City, March 2009

ARMANDO **ROMERO**

was born in Mexico City in 1964, and studied at the National School of Painting, Sculpture and Printmaking also known as "La Esmeralda," in Mexico City. He taught art history, design and drawing at the College Center for Studies in Science and Communications in Mexico City in 1991. Romero taught sculpture, painting and art history at La Esmeralda from 1991 through 1997. He lives and works in Mexico City.

SELECTED SOLO EXHIBITIONS

XX Century Parade, simultaneously presented at Leslie Feely Fine Art, New York, New York; The MAC, Dallas, Texas; and Tasende Gallery, Los Angeles, 2009

Amazing Animals in Danger of Extinction, Galerie Espacio, Morges, Switzeland, 2008

The History of Secret Worlds, Alpha Gallery, Boston, Massachusetts, 2008

Vandalism and Other Irreverences, Tasende Gallery, West Hollywood and La Jolla, California, 2007

Saintly Landscapes, Galería Drexel, Monterrey, Nuevo León, México, 2006

History of a Circus That Never Existed, Galerie Espacio, Morges, Switzerland, 2005

The Painter's Workshop, Galería Casa Colón, Mérida, Yucatán, México, 2004

The Garden of Delights, University Cultural Center, Morelia, Michoacán, México, 2003

A Long History in Small Acts, Galerie Espacio, Morges, Switzerland, 2003

New Painting of Armando Romero, Loft 523, New Orleans, Louisiana, 2002

Saints and Heroes, Galería Casa Colón, Mérida, Yucatán, México, 2002

Reversed World, Galerie Espacio, Morges, Switzerland, 2001

Secret World, Macay Museum, Mérida, Yucatán, México, 2001

New Paintings, Galería Casa Colón, Miami, Florida, 2001

The New Temptations of St. Anthony, Cloister University of Sor Juana, Mexico City, México, 2000

The Dream Labyrinth, University Hospital of Geneva, Geneva, Switzerland, 2000

Beyond Dreams, Galerie Espacio, Morges, Switzerland, 2000

Museum el Centenario, San Pedro Garza García, Nuevo León, México, 1999

Notes on Defining Painting, Galería Drexel, Monterrey, Nuevo León, México, 1998

ENPEG "La Esmeralda" Gallery, Mexico City, México, 1992

Casa de la Cultura de Tlalpan, Tlalpan, México, 1989